The Art of Display

Katherine Sorrell

The Art of Display

creating style with decorative objects

MITCHELL BEAZLEY

First published in Great Britain in 2002 by Mitchell Beazley, an imprint of
Octopus Publishing Group Limited, 2-4 Heron Quays, London E14 4JP

Commissioning Editor: Emma Clegg
Executive Art Editor: Auberon Hedgecoe
Senior Editor: Lara Maiklem
Designer: Peggy Sadler
Picture Researcher: Sarah Hopper
Copy Editor: Anne McDowall
Proofreader: Colette Campbell
Indexer: Penelope Kent
Production Controller: Angela Couchman

ISBN 1 84000 579 3

A CIP catalogue record for this book is available from the British Library

Typeset in DIN
Produced by Toppan Printing Co. (HK) Ltd.
Printed and bound in China

contents

introduction

To create a beautiful display of objects is a natural instinct – after all, what's the point of owning lovely things if you don't show them off? But making a display can be full of pitfalls. Choosing the right objects, finding a good spot in which to place them, coordinating shapes, sizes, and colours, providing flattering lighting; all these issues need to be considered carefully. Yet the process can be hugely enjoyable and the results endlessly rewarding.

It is probable that man has always made attempts, however rudimentary, to display his possessions in some way. As Alistair McAlpine writes in *Collecting and Display*, "People have been living with their collections for centuries. The ancient Greeks collected Oriental carpets, wall hangings and ornate furniture from Persia to display in their homes; during the Renaissance, whole rooms were given over to 'cabinets of curiosities'; members of the English middle class of the eighteenth century filled their great halls with cartloads of artwork from Europe. Today, we continue to use our living space to display collected treasures."

So why do we display things? At one time it may have been to evoke religious awe, to confer status, or to gain respect; today we may wish to give ourselves the satisfaction of showing off our beautiful things, provide pleasure for visitors, or simply enhance the decor of a room. Displays add character and individuality and often become a focal point. They can even be used to draw the eye away from flaws elsewhere, adding a layer of interest in a dull room and providing colour, form, and texture in a lifeless area.

And it's not only the choice of objects that makes or breaks a display: the means by which they are arranged can often be just as important, so that an intriguing arrangement of inexpensive or found items will often have a greater impact than a predictable display of very valuable pieces. Some displays work as if by magic; others, though they may try very hard, just don't get it right. It is hard to explain why this may be, because (perhaps unfortunately) there are no hard and fast rules, no instant solutions. There are, however, some basic principles and helpful suggestions, which can enable you to create attractive and inspiring displays.

What do you want to achieve?

The first thing you will need to think about is what you would like the display to achieve. Generally, the aim will be to highlight the aesthetic qualities of the objects as much as possible, while complementing the decoration of your home and not overwhelming other furnishings. More specifically, however, do you want to show off a single object in a dramatic way, or to display a group of objects? If the display is to contain more than one object, would you like them to be seen as one entity, a series of coordinating pieces, or a multitude of collectibles? Do you want the display to focus on colour, form, or material? Should it look inviting, so that guests may wish to pick up the objects and inspect them closely, or would you prefer it to be more formal and distant? There are all sorts of choices and it is best to be clear about the answers to such questions before you start.

◀◀ (Page 7) In the home of one of Britain's leading interior designers, identical accessories are displayed on simple shelves in neat, uniform rows, creating an effect that is at once formal and modern.

◀ Effective displays do not have to be imposing or expensive. Here, plain forms and toning colours add up to a look that's attractive, uncomplicated and easy-going.

▶ In coordinating colours and graduating sizes, these cushions have been carefully arranged to create an appealingly subtle and sophisticated display.

Looking for inspiration

There are various places you can look for extra inspiration. Art galleries and museums have refined the art of display and may provide some clues as to where to begin, though their exact solutions will often be rather formal, expensive, or on too large a scale. Shop windows, too, are a great place to look; their purpose is to have their contents look as great as possible so that people will buy them, and the results are often innovative and exciting. While such approaches cannot always be translated directly into a domestic context, they may offer a starting point for your own ideas. Looking through books and magazines is another easy way to gain inspiration. Cut pictures out of magazines and collect a scrapbook showing interesting displays – it may prove

◄ Using mirroring and repetition is a good way to add interest to a display. This example is utterly pared down, but the silhouettes made by the pair of 1950s dishes are intriguing and unusual.

► The high gloss of these polished stone eggs makes a beauliful contrast to the soft, warm glow of the wooden panelling behind.

invaluable. And, of course, when you visit friends' homes take a good look at what they've done and ask them how they achieved it. Be open to influences from nature, too: a walk on the beach might reveal a wonderful arrangement of driftwood that's been thrown onto the sand by the sea, or on a stroll through the park you may notice combinations of natural colours that you would never have thought of putting together. Creating a beautiful display is just as much about being guided by instinct and emotion as by a set of rules.

Making the most of what you have

With a few ideas in mind, you will probably then find that the shape and size of your objects and of your room will start to dictate the form of the display. There will be certain combinations that either suggest themselves naturally or that simply will not work. If you are decorating the entire room, consider the display at the same time as you are choosing paint colours, fabric, furniture, and, importantly, lighting. All these elements will need to fit together harmoniously in order to establish the ideal effect. If the room is quite formal, a strictly symmetrical display of traditional objects will probably best suit it, while a low-key look might be complemented by an informal assortment of subtle, natural objects, or a glamorous, opulent room by an over-the-top array of glittering, eye-catching pieces.

When putting the display together, pay attention to both the detail and the bigger picture. It's important to stand right back and get an overview of what it looks like, and also to be

◄ Even a handful of rounded stones thrown into an olive dish can make a pretty display, thanks to careful attention to their similarity in size and gentle colours.

precise in terms of arrangements and positioning. Experiment and change things around; most displays don't need to be permanently fixed, and after living with it for a while you may feel a different arrangement would be better.

Sir Terence Conran, in *Easy Living*, writes, "It takes a certain leap of faith to buy and display what really moves you, but the result will give you pleasure on a daily basis, and imbue your home with personality." Whatever your choice of objects or means of display, try not to make the finished result overly formal or perfect: this is, after all, your home not a gallery, and the display should reflect your personality and preferences. Sometimes the best method is to throw all conventions aside and do something unexpected. If you like the result and love to live with it, that's all that matters.

▲ Displays can be squeezed into all sorts of interesting corners. In this country sitting room, an apparently impromptu display of old wooden spoons breaks up the square outlines of pictures and bookshelves.

▲ Lighting plays a huge part in the effectiveness of a display. Backlighting items with strong silhouettes – in this case five identical, unusually shaped bottles – is one way to ensure that they stand out dramatically.

▶ Contemporary displays often combine the simple with the surprising – for example the plain vases with artichokes shown here. Regular, well-spaced positioning is all part of the look.

single objects

When Modernist architect Ludwig Mies van der Rohe said, famously, "Less is more", he probably wasn't thinking about the display of a single object in a room. Nevertheless, his rule applies in this context: the opportunities for making an impact with just one fabulous object are endless.

Before you decide how and where to display a single object, first consider just why you have chosen it and what you want to achieve with the display. Sometimes you may need to take one item away from a group display because it doesn't look right with the other pieces, yet still warrants being shown off elsewhere. Or perhaps you feel that a particularly prized object deserves all the attention and so should be set dramatically on its own. In this case think about what it is that makes the piece so special and ensure that this aspect – its colour, texture, form, provenance, or whatever – is emphasized. Perhaps the display area is quite small, and so it would be best to display only one item there; or perhaps your aim is to add excitement to the room with a single eye-catching object that cannot fail to be noticed.

Having thought these things through, the next step is to consider the object itself. Think about its size, shape, colour, and texture: whether the object is small or large, flat or three-dimensional, angular or organic in shape, vividly coloured or muted and subtle, strongly textured or smooth, will all have a bearing on how you create your display. Just as important is the style of the piece: is it an antique or a contemporary piece? Is it ethnic in origin or style?

Large objects

Displaying a single large object makes a striking statement – not only about the piece itself, but also about yourself, your taste, and your style. This type of display would most obviously consist of a classical sculpture, an impressive painting, an oversized ceramic piece, or perhaps a superb example of handblown glass. Think laterally, however, and there are many more things that can be used to create a marvellous single-object display: a Japanese kimono, for example, or an African mask; a classic twentieth-century chair or stool that's too valuable to be sat on but has a form that's really worth studying; a massively enlarged photograph of a flowerhead, hung banner-like on a wall; a giant cushion with detailed embroidery, appliqué, or beading; a Venetian glass mirror; a light fitting that's a work of art in itself; a garden urn filled with dried grasses; a hand-tufted rug with bold, colourful patterning; even a plant with a highly sculptural shape... the list could go on and on.

It is vital to consider scale when positioning a large object – this type of display needs a generous amount of room in order to be noticed. Ensure that it doesn't overwhelm its surroundings by giving it space to "breathe" on a large wall or floor area, a big cabinet, a wide shelf, or whatever. To avoid the impression that the room is crammed full of stuff, and to ensure that the object can be seen clearly, it's best to keep furniture reasonably far away. That said, there are times when it's fun to play with scale and put a large object in a small room for a deliberate effect. If

◀ ◀ (Page 17) This artwork by the Boyle Family dominates an airy, modern conservatory, its rough texture contrasting emphatically with the smooth, shiny glass and steel that surround it.

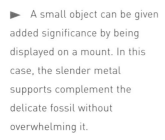

▶ A small object can be given added significance by being displayed on a mount. In this case, the slender metal supports complement the delicate fossil without overwhelming it.

you want to try this, it's a good idea to link the piece visually with other things in the room, either through colour, texture, or form, so that it fits with the feel of the furnishings rather than being simply a bizarre addition. This sort of bold approach can work marvellously, or can sometimes fail dismally, but don't be afraid to experiment with scale in this way if the idea intrigues you.

Small objects

Size really does matter here. The smaller an object, the harder it is to display on its own – anything smaller than, say, an average-sized vase, runs the risk of being lost among the general furnishings of most rooms. That said, you can create lovely surprises by placing the occasional small object in an unexpected place: a plaster cast of a fern

hung low on a wall, in a corner next to an armchair where the sitter can admire it, perhaps; a beaded corsage between two rows of books on a shelf; an egg-shaped ceramic vessel perched on the corner of a coffee table; or maybe a chintz-printed cup and saucer tucked into a whitewashed niche.

The key to successfully displaying a small single object is scale. Get it right and differences in scale won't be noticeable; get it wrong and the display will look and feel uncomfortable. A small object, whether a watercolour, a bud vase, a fossil, a fragment of fabric, a pebble, a wine glass, a folded-paper sculpture, a dried leaf, a glass paperweight, or a silver napkin ring, needs to be "framed", either literally or metaphorically, by its surroundings. Generally, a small picture is given a relatively small frame, and the same goes for three-dimensional objects, too, the "frame", in this case,

◄ Positioned on a wall in the corner of this bedroom, a cello provides elegant, curving lines that subtly offset the square planes elsewhere in the room and the straight lines created by the neck, tailpiece, and bow.

being the area in which the object is displayed – a portion of wall or floor space, the top of a table, a shelf, or a cabinet. Put a small object in a large space and it will look foolish, lost, and out of place; put it in a smaller space – maybe a specially designed cabinet or niche, a side table rather than a coffee table, or a plinth rather than a long, wide shelf – and it will demand an appreciative glance and a closer look.

Making an impact

Whether a single object is large or small, there are many ways in which it can make a really superb display. One is to ensure that it works brilliantly with the room in which it is set – the proportions, architectural style, shapes, colours, textures, and furnishings. Choose whether to complement these features by displaying an object that blends well with them, creating a feeling of harmony, calmness, and sophistication, or to create a strong contrast by using a piece that has very different features. A modern piece in a period room can look stunning, for example, as can an antique in a contemporary room. A curvy piece can really soften a space that has lots of angular lines, while a linear, geometric object will have more of an impact in a room where other furnishings are more curvilinear. Similarly, a smooth, shiny wall or table (perhaps made of stainless steel, glass, polished plaster, or lacquer) makes a wonderful backdrop for a roughly textured wood or stone carving, while strong colour contrasts always ensure that a display stands out from its surroundings.

◄ Although this romantic birdcage makes a superb impact all on its own, it also works perfectly in its setting, its intricate, filigree wirework complementing the delicate embroidery of the curtains.

► Positioning a huge urn filled with tall grasses in front of a window serves to emphasize its size, shape and texture, particularly when, as here, the room is otherwise minimally decorated.

A single object may be displayed on a shelf or in a cabinet, at the end of the sofa, beside the bed, on a turn in the landing, in the corner of a patio, above the kitchen sink, or on a plinth in the hall. But wherever you position it, such a display often benefits from having plenty of surrounding space, either to give room for the eye to wander, or for the viewer literally to walk around the piece and appreciate it from all angles. If you have a three-dimensional object but no room to do this, you could simply fit a mirror behind it to double its impact. The means by which your eye is led to the piece is important, too: there may be a way in which you can create a vista – through use of colour or arrangement of furnishings – that draws the viewer irresistibly in, so that the beauty of the piece is unmissable.

◄ A beautifully carved bust: a classic example of the single-object display in a traditional setting. The effect is subtle and sophisticated.

► An elegantly carved wooden swan is just the right size for this narrow windowsill, and fits wonderfully with the view through the glass.

Classical or contemporary?

Single-object displays are often statement pieces, and can set the style for an entire room. You may possess a beautiful, traditional object – a classical bust or a landscape painting, a tapestry or an ancient urn – that's been passed down the family from generation to generation, or that you came across in an antiques shop or an auction. Or you may be a collector of contemporary craft, and wish to show off a wood-carving, an unusual glass sculpture, or a woven-plastic basket. In each case you need to decide how much you wish your display to dominate its setting and provide a focal point. Placing a classical piece in a traditional room is,

of course, subtle and smart; the feel will be harmonious and sophisticated. And contemporary pieces placed in modern contexts will, again, blend beautifully and speak volumes about your individual style. For heightened drama, however, you could try juxtaposing old and new, creating clashing contrasts between the centuries. On a Georgian bookshelf, for example, you could stand a curvy, modern ceramic vase, or on a traditional Windsor chair you could prop a cushion embroidered with sparkling sequins. Alternatively, in a minimal bedroom you could hang an oil painting in an elaborate gilt frame, or, under the glass top of a modern coffee table, place a Victorian collection of butterflies.

groups

Andy Warhol said that "anything goes with anything", and the most inspired decorators do seem to be able to group all sorts of things together and come up with a display that creates a fabulous impression. There's no doubt that objects massed together can have great impact, and group displays can be both satisfying to create and enormously effective. Even the most unprepossessing of objects carries a certain weight when displayed in a group, and this sort of display is also ideal if some of the pieces are not exactly perfect, or if the items are individually not of great value or importance. The end result can be much greater than the sum of the parts.

A group display may consist of almost anything; it may be a collection of differing objects or a set of identical items: a series of Delftware plates or tiles; a dozen framed silk headscarves; pebbles in graduating sizes; mirrored baubles placed with crystal droplets; wooden hat moulds; woven-willow and metal boxes; a row of modern chairs in bonbon shades, or a set of engraved wine glasses and matching decanters. Having decided on what you wish to display, the shapes, sizes, and colours of the objects will start to dictate the way in which you arrange them. The rest is a mix of instinct, experiment, and following a few basic principles.

Arranging pairs

Displays of identical pairs of objects are probably the most simple, and often the most visually powerful, of all. Whether it's a pair of silver candlesticks or two raffia-and-wood lamps, there's something extremely pleasing about this mirroring and doubling. The only prerequisite is that you really do need to make sure they're placed evenly and symmetrically – if you're not confident about judging by eye, there's nothing wrong with using a tape measure.

Pairs that aren't identical can make a marvellous display, too – a couple of pine cones picked up on a country walk, two postcards in similar colours but with different images, or two hand-made baskets of the same pattern but in contrasting shades, for instance. As long as they are similar enough, they can be displayed in the same way as an identical pair, but with a less formal, more contemporary look. However, it is harder to create a link between two very dissimilar objects, and it may be necessary to add another piece in order to provide a better balance.

Trios and small groups

The visual "weight" of an object is hugely important when arranging groups. An object made of clear glass will appear more fragile, delicate, and "light" than one of identical size and shape that is made of white ceramic, for example. Arranging them as a symmetrical pair will look odd. Give more weight to the glass object by placing something else with it in order to balance the display. In the same way, two tall, thin objects will balance one tall, wide one; a couple of small paintings will balance another, larger one; and so on. This principle applies to all group displays, and with practice it becomes second-nature to apply.

Groups of three make very satisfying displays and are easy to arrange. If the heights of the objects vary, the simplest approach will be to place the tallest piece at the back, with the two others in front and to each side. If they are the same height but different shapes, you might place them in a row, creating a subtle interplay between the order of the display and the variety of forms.

A group of at least five objects that are identical or very similar can create a fantastically impressive display, the repetition utterly simple in itself but visually very striking. A tightly packed row of even the most ordinary objects looks amazing. The Pop Artists of the 1960s were masters of this – think of Andy Warhol's paintings of Campbell's soup cans for the basic idea. Even a row of lemons or limes along a windowsill, or pearly sea shells along the edge of a bath, will make a much greater impact than you might imagine.

When objects vary in only one sense – maybe colour, or height, or texture – they can be displayed ranging from the tallest to the smallest, the palest to the darkest, the busiest to the simplest, or the roughest to the smoothest, creating a subtle transition that has gentle coherence. Or they can be alternated in a way that creates a rhythm of recurring patterns for a more dynamic, energetic display. And remember, it is always best to display an uneven number of objects – it is generally accepted that even numbers are subliminally less appealing to look at.

◄◄ (Page 27) In group displays the end result is often greater than the sum of the parts. A carefully arranged selection of pebbles, for example, creates a setting that is contemplative, calm, and coolly effective.

◄ The shape and colour of these three vases filled with plants are satisfyingly repetitive – a beautifully simple display.

► Even the most ordinary objects can make a powerful impression when arranged en masse. Here, useful storage is also an imaginative focal point.

Symmetry and asymmetry

Every time you display more than one object, you will need to make a decision as to whether to opt for symmetry or asymmetry. The former is almost always easier to get right. Edith Wharton and Ogden Codman Jr defined symmetry as "the sanity of decoration", and wrote, in *The Decoration of Houses*, "The desire for symmetry, for balance, for rhythm in form as well as in sound, is one of the most inveterate of human instincts." Indeed, symmetry has been important to us since the days of the ancient Greeks, signifying reflection, equilibrium, regularity, the notion of beauty in humans, architecture, and design. So symmetrical displays generally appear more classical, considered, and refined, at ease in their sense of perfection. Asymmetrical displays, on the other hand, can look more modern, spontaneous, intuitive, and unselfconscious. When an asymmetrical display works, it looks superb, offering intrigue, dynamism, and a sort of imperfect beauty that can be incredibly appealing.

Which type you choose will depend partly on the objects you are planning to display, but a great deal will also rest on your confidence and skill, and the effect that you wish to create. Symmetrical displays tend to suit traditional rooms – the Georgian period, in particular, emphasised the rules of symmetry. Assymetry, on the other hand, is ideal for making an impact in a contemporary space, and suits the current vogue for displays that don't look too prepared or static.

▶ A row of slim, straight vases makes an absolutely pared-down display. Its powerful effect comes largely from their strict alignment and repetition of form and also from their transparency, which works well with the minimalist setting.

Linking objects together

One important principle in selecting items for a group display is to establish the link between them. This may or may not be immediately obvious, but there is usually some logic behind even the most apparently chaotic displays.

Look first for physical characteristics that create dynamic comparisons or contrasts between the objects. The most obvious are shape, size, colour, and texture. A series of objects that demonstrate strong vertical lines, that have cubic or spherical shapes, or possess strong angles, for example, may form repetitive patterns that look attractive, whether or not the objects are identical to each other.

Size matters, but there's also the question of proportion. Sizes may differ, sometimes dramatically, but the proportions of the various objects to each other should always be attractive. One way of ensuring that this is the case is to work

on the basis of a mathematical relationship known as the Fibonacci series, named after its creator, Leonardo Fibonacci, a thirteenth-century Italian mathematician. In this sequence, each measurement is the sum of the previous two. So if, say, you were displaying a row of lacquered boxes, they might increase in length from 1cm (0.4in) to 2cm (0.8in), then 3cm (1.2in), 5cm (2in), 8cm (3.2in), 13cm (5.2in), and so on, and perhaps decreasing again in the same proportions. As Paul Zelanski and Mary Pat Fisher point out in *The Art of Seeing*, this sequencing is found in nature, too, for example in the chambers in a nautilus shell, which grow in increasing, spiralling Fibonacci patterns. If it works in nature, it can work in a man-made display in just the same way.

Another means of producing pleasing proportions in a group display is to use the Ancient Greek system known as the "golden rectangle", in which the length of the short side

▶ The effect of this display is quite different from the symmetrical one shown opposite. A looser, more casual look has been achieved here simply by placing these pretty tealight holders into an asymmetrical pattern.

to the long side of a rectangle is 1:1.618. This figure was believed to be the most attractive proportion, and was almost certainly used in the building of the Egyptian pyramids. Try measuring it out if you wish; however, once you start placing objects in a display you may very well find that you have hit this ideal proportion anyway – certainly the Greeks believed that all humans had an innate sense of it.

Yet another method is to follow the idea of "harmonic" proportion, which relates to musical chords that are made up of tones that have vibration frequencies with simple ratios such as 2:3, 3:4 and 4:5. This notion was used by the

◄ A smooth graduation of colour and variation in height gives this collection of curvaceous glass vases a pleasing, gentle dynamism.

▲ An unusual display of decorated snowboards allows for a studied repetition of shapes contrasted with exciting variations in pattern and colour.

► Why hide attractive accessories in a cupboard? Hanging your handbags in an ad hoc fashion not only makes a decorative display, but also allows easy access when you want to use them.

classical architect Andrea Palladio and, more recently, by the Modernist architect Le Corbusier.

Colour can be one of the strongest ways of linking objects together in a display. You may wish to concentrate on clashing differences or coordinating similarities, or to graduate through various tones of the same shade, or to move from light to dark or vice versa. And texture plays an important role as well – it's been called "the new colour". By contrasting textures, even in a display of objects of similar colour, you can create subtle and appealing impact.

Any group display will appear more coherent if size, shape, proportion, colour, and texture are considered, but don't forget that what you leave out can be as important as what you put in. However much you love them, some objects may simply not fit into the group, and it's always best to remove them and, if possible, display them elsewhere.

Finally, don't forget that sometimes the reason for grouping certain objects may be a purely personal one – paintings by artists from the same area but different periods, for example, or mementoes from foreign travels. These group displays tend to come together with ease, having been chosen by someone with a particular taste. Nevertheless, it is worth taking care to arrange them in a way that creates a harmonious result.

◄ Some collections benefit from a tight grouping. These brightly painted tin toys, for example, are packed together on glass shelves in order to increase their impact.

▼ These little cherubs have been hung informally to make a natural pattern that could easily become part of the background, rather like an ornate wallpaper.

Large collections

The true collector tends to amass vast numbers of objects (from stamps to shoes, marbles to Ming vases), which, if they're not to be put away out of sight, need careful arrangement so as not to overwhelm an ordinary home. One obvious solution is to dedicate an entire room, lined with shelves or cabinets, to the display. Where this is not feasible, however, some lateral thinking is necessary. If space is really limited, one answer is to store a large part of the collection and create a small display area in which objects can be swapped for those in storage on a regular basis. Otherwise, space will have to be found in unexpected places:

There are plenty of occasions when objects on display work best propped casually against a wall. This grouping of antique cheese graters, leant against a rustic wooden wall, for example, is delightfully impromptu.

perhaps on shelves ranged high up around the room, or in niches set into the thickness of the walls, or on the backs of doors, or in piles of glass-fronted boxes (see pages 108-119, for more ideas on unusual methods of display).

When a collection is of a more manageable size, it can make a wonderful display that adds life and character to any room. With objects that are very similar in shape, size, or colour, a simple display in regular rows is easy to achieve and has great visual authority. More tricky to arrange are lots of objects that are all quite different. Here, the solution is to approach the display as though you were setting up a still life for an artist, considering the focal point or points, the interplay of form, colour, and texture, and the overall

outlines created by the arrangement. Another method is to treat the collection like a window display in a shop, where, similarly, the aim is to group different objects together in the most attractive way possible. Look for connections in shape, size, and colour, and aim for a display that emphasizes these to create coherence and calm, rather than visual dissonance. Mary Portas, in *Windows, the Art of Retail Display*, says that while sometimes less is more, she also believes in the premise that "more is more", adding that in a slightly chaotic display "the eye is distracted over many areas and it's a feast of layers and elements of surprise – every time you come back you see something new". Such layering of objects comes with practice, but will give many hours of pleasure.

► A collection of flat objects can make an intriguing display when wall-mounted in an unexpected environment. Here, an unusual collection of antique wooden combs is protected by an acrylic sheet so as to form a splashback behind a basin.

Positioning a group display

Having selected the items you want to display together, you should begin to look at the shapes they make as a group – at the geometrical structure of the display as a whole. It is helpful to think in terms of blocks, such as squares or rectangles, lines, and triangles. Triangles will usually point upward – think, for example, of a picture hung over a fireplace with two objects placed on either side of the mantelpiece – but can actually be any way up. Try to see the things you have chosen as outlines or silhouettes rather than as objects in their own right. The easiest way to do this is to step back from the display and half-close your eyes. This will help you to gain an overview of the shape the objects make when placed together, and your display is more likely to have a thoughtful rationale that will give it cohesion.

When placing a number of different objects together, start by positioning one or two of the stronger, most striking pieces first. These will often be the largest, but not always. It makes sense to put taller pieces at the back. Fill in the gaps with the medium and smaller pieces, working toward a flow of shapes, a strong geometrical structure, a variety of heights, and an emphasis on the most intriguing characteristics. If necessary, add variety to the heights by placing one or more pieces on a mount, and bear in mind that if a piece jars with others in the group, it is best to remove it and display it separately.

horizontal surfaces

Placing objects on top of a flat surface is the simplest, most obvious, and often the most effective method of creating a display. From shelving to windowsills, mantelpieces to tables, pedestals to the tops of wardrobes, there is a huge range of flat surfaces that will form a fabulous home for large collections, small groups, or dramatic single objects.

Displays on flat surfaces can be very poised and deliberate, even rather grand – a pair of silver candlesticks on a Georgian mantelpiece, for example, or a perfectly positioned row of Oriental vases on a black lacquer shelf. But they can also be delightfully informal, such as a small group of cut-glass perfume bottles on the side of a dressing table, or some smooth pebbles scattered on the windowsill next to a bath. Even a pile of hardback art books on a coffee table makes its own attractive display. This is the beauty of flat surfaces: they can be so unassuming in their own right that you don't notice them, but they are incredibly versatile and easy to work with. When you take the time to develop a thoughtful display the results are full of impact and appeal.

Shelves

Shelves are the workhorses of the display world. As well as providing an ideal method of displaying all sorts of objects, whether books or ceramics, glassware or woodwork, stone or metalware, they are also an efficient means of storage, usually taking up a minimal amount of space and offering little, if any, decorative distraction.

Shelves can be built in practically any space around the house, in obvious places such as rectangular alcoves beside a chimney breast or along the back wall of a home office, or in unusual or intriguing positions that can provide useful solutions when space is short – above a door, between two windows, in a stairwell, or inside a disused fireplace, for example. Shelves can be built across a corner or made to snake around a curved surface; they can be built as sets on which to display a mass of objects, or singly for a more sparse and modern appearance.

Contemporary shelving tends toward the plain and simple – functionality at its purest. Thick boards of painted medium-density fibreboard (MDF) with hidden supports are one way to achieve this look. Sheets of glossy plate glass, supported on minimal brackets, are ideal for displaying delicate items, such as glassware or porcelain. Alternatively, a solid shelf made from a gorgeously grained wood (such as oak, walnut, zebrano, or wenge), or covered with a thin wood veneer, will make its presence known in a sophisticated, richly coloured interior. If your decor is more traditional, consider wrought iron, gilding, and decorative mouldings, or cover the shelves with leather, painted motifs, or patterned fabric or wallpaper.

While the total amount of shelving you install will depend on the wall space available and how many items you wish to display (and whether or not your collection is likely to grow in the future), the length and depth of the shelves will depend on both practical and visual considerations. A short

◄◄ (Page 41) A matching chair and table with objects displayed under glass take on an artistic, almost surreal appearance. This is an innovative and eye-catching method that cannot fail to be a talking point.

► Slim shelves are a useful way of displaying photographs, paintings, and prints, and are particularly effective when they span the length of a room. This large collection is unified by a black-and-white theme.

► In this clean-lined room, a wooden shelf echoes in shape and style the console table below it. The artworks placed on it, though overlapping, are arranged quite formally for a calm, sophisticated feel.

shelf running across a long wall can look strangely curtailed, although a series of short shelves placed at regular intervals may provide an intriguing variation on the norm. On a narrow stretch of wall you could build short shelves above each other in a ladder-like way, while in large rooms it is often better to be bold with shelving and fit long, confident runs, remembering that the thickness of the shelving should be relative to its length, or it will appear spindly and mean (and may not be strong enough). Extra-deep shelves will need more supports (and don't forget the weight of the objects that will be put on them), while slim shelves are ideal in small rooms and can provide the perfect display area for

rows of tiny objects, or for propped-up books or pictures. And if you wish to make a real impact with your shelves, eliminate clutter and display only a small number of clean-lined pieces – or even nothing at all, letting the form and surface finish of the shelf speak beautifully for itself.

Mantelpieces

A fireplace is often the focal point of a room, so it follows that a skilful arrangement of objects above it will draw the eye and create a striking display – which is why the mantelpiece is a traditional, and often used, location for special pieces. While conventional displays on a mantelpiece

◄ Although these shelves are very full, their contents have been arranged in a neat and orderly fashion, with consideration to variations in colour and scale.

might include vases, bottles, clocks, and candelabra, unusual things can also look amazing here: some lateral thinking might perhaps suggest objects such as African masks, beaded and sequinned baubles, china jelly moulds, Moroccan tea glasses, pieces of driftwood, or even plastic toys or neon signs.

Much will depend on the decor of the room, and particularly of the fireplace and its surround. A classic room with an ornate marble fireplace will be complemented by a calm, symmetrical arrangement of sophisticated, traditional items, positioned at carefully measured distances. A contemporary room with a minimal fireplace, on the other hand, may cry out for a collection of less serious objects, placed more randomly and loosely. Modern rooms usually benefit from displays with plenty of space around them, while the traditional look tends to be a little more cluttered. Bear in mind, as well, that the size, shape, and number of objects on display should relate to the proportions of the fireplace and the visual weight of its surround. Avoid placing huge items on a small mantelpiece, and vice versa, or overpowering a narrow mantelpiece with a crowded collection of objects.

▲ Even inexpensive items such as postcards can make an attractive display. These are linked by a simple theme and propped up neatly on a plain mantelpiece.

▶ Each object in this charming decorative arrangement has the same "feel", in terms of soft colour, organic shape, and rough texture.

When considering what to display on a mantelpiece, remember that you can also play around with materials and surface textures; it may be nice to contrast the soft sheen of marble with rough, angular bark, for example, or to show highly polished glassware on roughly cast concrete – such subtle changes of texture, often not obvious at first glance, do make a real difference to the impact of a display.

Windowsills

Putting objects on a windowsill is almost inevitably an informal means of display, and as such can be utterly appealing. The effect is almost as if they are there by chance, so their discovery is a delightful, intriguing surprise.

This type of display suits objects that aren't terribly grand (and not too precious, either, as things on a windowsill can be quite vulnerable to accidents). Things made from natural materials are ideal, such as turned wooden bowls, shells, pebbles, bunches of twigs, baskets, driftwood, and fossils. Small hand-made ceramics can also look lovely, as can chintz cups and saucers, or hand-beaten pewter but glass, in any form, will always be an absolutely appropriate choice, as this is the ideal place for bright natural light to illuminate its glorious colours or engraved patterning.

Windowsills can be used for attractive displays in any room, from the kitchen to the bathroom, the hallway to the living room, the dining room to a turn in the stairs. Pick

◄◄ Softly coloured paintings of shells and coral make a strong diagonal line, complemented by a relaxed grouping of the real thing. The two- and three-dimensional objects work together, thanks to a set of mini easels.

◄ A dramatic difference in height makes this an attention-grabbing display. The twining plant forms are enhanced by the hazy light shining through the window.

▶ This unusual, hexagonal shelving system could almost be a display in itself. Each space is ideal for showing off an individual, medium-sized object. Most of the items on display here are attractive pieces of kitchen equipment.

▶▶ This haphazard display of pieces, with multiple layers of books, magazines and china along the depth and height of the shelves, carries an air of eccentric charm.

objects that complement the other furnishings of the room in a low-key way, scattering them in an accidental fashion for a quiet display that is simple and charming.

Arranging displays on narrow surfaces

Because there is a physical limit to the depth of most shelves, mantelpieces, and windowsills, displays on these types of flat surfaces are governed by an upper limit to the size of the pieces used. It will always look awkward if the base of an object juts out beyond the edge of the surface that it is standing on. Conversely, tiny items may well look lost in this type of display – a little trial and error will soon

demonstrate the possible sizes, bearing in mind that a number of small pieces will have the same visual weight as just one larger piece.

The obvious way of arranging objects on a long, thin surface is in a row, whether it be an ordered line of identical pieces, a gathering of similarly sized and shaped pieces, or an eclectic mix that works together in a more random fashion, perhaps in terms of colour, size, material, form, or provenance. First decide whether you wish to spread your pieces out evenly or stand them closely together, and then look at the outline that they make against their background, especially their relative heights – it is generally best to avoid

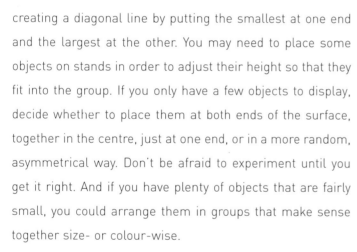

◀ Against an austere backdrop, the dappled colours and intriguing textures of these objects come to the fore. The informality of their arrangement suits their modest nature.

▶ A large tabletop is perfect for displays of objects of disparate size and height. A surface where flat objects are displayed should be low enough for you to look down over them.

creating a diagonal line by putting the smallest at one end and the largest at the other. You may need to place some objects on stands in order to adjust their height so that they fit into the group. If you only have a few objects to display, decide whether to place them at both ends of the surface, together in the centre, just at one end, or in a more random, asymmetrical way. Don't be afraid to experiment until you get it right. And if you have plenty of objects that are fairly small, you could arrange them in groups that make sense together size- or colour-wise.

When arranging books, there is much to be said for displaying them, too, in order of either colour or size – you will be amazed how much more dramatic and cohesive they look than when randomly placed. Of course, books needn't take up an entire shelf: the occasional gap can be filled with a three-dimensional piece that breaks up their square outlines, or the shelf can be left empty to provide a visual breathing space. Or, place books flat on the shelves with a space between each pile – they take up no more room and the display makes a refreshing change.

Finally, do not under estimate the importance of the background to a shelf or mantelpiece. The colour of a painted wall or chimney breast, its texture or material, can enhance or detract from what is displayed on the surface in front of it. Depending on the objects that you are displaying, a neutral background may be the ideal way in which to make things stand out; or it may be better to use a vivid colour that either picks out a shade from your display or contrasts boldly with it. Alternatively, use mirror to double the effect of what's on show.

Tabletops and other flat surfaces

Coffee tables, side tables, console tables, square tables, round tables, semi-circular tables, long thin tables, low tables, high tables – all sorts of tables make the perfect resting place for a wide variety of displays. And don't forget the opportunities for placing things on the tops of cabinets, wardrobes, pianos, boxes, chair seats, or stools or indeed any other flat surface that happens to provide a handy resting place.

◄ In a corner of the art gallery at Kettle's Yard, Cambridge, England, mottled sunlight falls upon an artful arrangement of rounded pebbles, proving that a satisfying display can be made from the simplest of things.

The undisputed master of displays on tables, and in fact the instigator of this particular method of display, was the twentieth-century English decorator David Hicks. Hicks was renowned for what came to be known as his "tablescapes", flat surfaces on which he grouped together just the right number and style of objects to form a work of art in its own right. Hicks mixed old and new with confidence, and was bold in his use of colour and pattern. "It isn't what you do – it's how you do it; it isn't what you possess, but how you make the most of it through the way in which you present and arrange it," he maintained. One of his most notable trademark tricks was to use clear acrylic cubes in various sizes on which to place objects within the tablescapes, thus adding visual weight and authority to what were sometimes inexpensive, everyday pieces.

The larger the horizontal surface area, then the more scope there is for decorative flair: a display on a good-sized side table or on the top of a fairly large cabinet could encompass a number of objects and become the focal point of a room (see both pictures opposite). Alternatively, one end of a coffee table could provide an opportunity for a small, informal display of chosen objects, leaving the rest of the tabletop free for drinks, books, ashtrays, television remote controls, and other such necessary or useful bits and pieces.

However large or small the area though, tabletops and other such wide, flat surfaces provide excellent opportunities for displays that could be modern or classic in style, consisting of objects of almost any type and arranged in infinite eye-catching ways.

► A sideboard such as this can provide a perfect opportunity for a two-tiered display. This one uses simple forms with monumental silhouettes. A display is made of the useful storage boxes, too.

▼ The elaborate style of this chest of drawers is matched by the display on top of it. Perfectly symmetrical, the objects are oversized for the area, which gives them a rather grand and imposing appearance.

Arranging displays on large, flat surfaces

The first consideration when arranging a display on top of a table, cabinet, wardrobe, or similar, is always its height. Will it be above or below the eye-level of a normal viewing position (which could be either sitting or standing)? If below, as is frequently the case, the impact made by the tops of the objects will be important: a group of circular vases with brightly glazed interiors is a good example, making a display that is both colourful and rhythmic in its repetition of shapes. Conversely, if the display will be above eye-level, it will be important to consider how the objects will appear when seen from below.

A variation in the heights of the pieces on display, as Hicks demonstrated so well, gives a dynamism and thoughtful elegance to objects that may well be relatively

◄ Displays don't have to be composed of expensive objects. On this mantelpiece, family photographs, a wine glass full of flowers from the garden, a clock, an old mirror and a simple mug are enough to create a pretty arrangement.

► Unconventional objects can be put to use as the basis for an inspiring display. The impact of this one comes from the stark contrast between the industrial heaters and the delicate, elegant glassware carefully placed on top of them.

unimportant. Don't be afraid to use supports to achieve this effect, whether clear acrylic, stone, metal, wood, or plastic – whatever complements the items on display. In some cases it may even be possible to balance one item on top of another. Look at the outline that the forms make when placed together – a pyramid is generally pleasing, as is a stepped, or ziggurat, shape. The occasional tall piece breaking out above the others can be intriguing, although avoid using pieces that are totally out of proportion or they will look as though they have crept into the wrong display.

Sometimes the simplest of displays creates the most impact in these situations: just three large candles on a sideboard, for example, or a pair of bottle vases at each end of a console. But tabletops and the like are an ideal place on which to display collections, too, or groupings of disparate objects. Work within the aesthetic of the room and in harmony with the style of objects on display; and never feel that a display of objects, once put in place, can never be changed. Experimentation and alteration is a large part of the fun of display: as David Hicks explained, "One of the most relaxing and pleasurable things in life, I think, is to rearrange ones books, one's pictures and one's smaller possessions. There is an almost never-ending series of arrangements and solutions."

Plinths, pedestals, and brackets

When you wish to display just one superb or intriguing object, a plinth, pedestal, or bracket, wall-mounted or placed on a flat surface, is the ideal way to do it, emphasizing its shape, material, colour, and overall design.

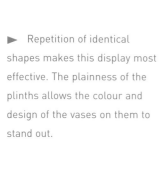
▶ Repetition of identical shapes makes this display most effective. The plainness of the plinths allows the colour and design of the vases on them to stand out.

Sometimes one plinth or a pair of plinths is enough; there may be occasions, however, when you could cover a wall or floor with a dramatic series of plinths that display a collection of pieces, as demonstrated above.

Plinths, pedestals, and other single stands should complement (and not distract from) the object that they display – for a minimal, modern room a simple box-shaped plinth made from painted medium-density fibreboard (MDF) creates an ideal surface on which to place almost any item. (See pages 128-9 for how to make one.) In other styles of room a more ornate plinth in a more expensive or unusual material might be appropriate, and there is an endless variety of things to choose from. Collector Alistair McAlpine

suggests terracotta drainage pipes, chimney pots, concrete wedges, railway sleepers, books, or even slabs of smooth-edged glass stacked at various angles, among other examples. Create a subtle contrast in colour, material, and texture between the plinth and the object on it, and it will draw the eye to give immense and impressive impact.

Finally, don't forget that you can also place objects on steps and staircases for unusual and dramatic effect. Choose the objects carefully, as they need to look good from both above and below, and don't crowd the stairs so much that they become impassable or dangerous. Avoid anything too delicate: pretty shoes, church candles, woven baskets, and carved-wooden figures are all interesting and practical.

◄ Even a staircase makes a
good surface for displays. Here,
an array of African figures
possesses rhythmic repetition
yet also subtle differences in
size and style.

cabinets & alcoves

Cabinets and cupboards, alcoves and niches, recesses and cubby holes – three-dimensional display areas are ideal for pieces that are particularly valuable and need protection, for showing off a really special item, or simply as a space-saving means of arranging a collection. Cabinets and alcoves act in the same way as a frame around a picture: they set the scene for your display, whether modern or traditional, boldly coloured or subtly neutral, and delineate its visual boundaries, large or small, deep or shallow. And just as frames and pictures must complement both each other and the room in which they're hung, so cabinets and their contents should, ideally, work together and fit well into their surroundings, creating an harmonious whole, giving the display maximum appeal.

The first cabinets evolved from the simple chests that were used to transport the possessions of medieval gentry when they moved from property to property. As cabinet-making developed almost into an art form, the furniture became more and more embellished, made from exotic woods, inlaid with marquetry, painted with elaborate scenes, or encrusted with jewels and precious metals. Indeed, it's not hard to imagine that the impact of the cabinet itself was often greater than the objects on show inside. Today, we tend to favour simplicity of style, so that the collection within the cabinet really shines – though that's not to say that cabinets must be boring or bland; they can, of course, be beautifully designed and made, elegantly detailed and highly attractive pieces in their own right.

As an alternative to free-standing cabinets, built-in cabinets or fitted units are often the perfect solution in a small or awkwardly shaped room, making the most of dead space and providing a range of custom-made display areas. Similarly, niches and recesses in the walls offer a wonderful opportunity for unexpected, eye-catching displays.

Fitted display areas

The architecture of many houses, whether old or new, lends itself perfectly to fitting cabinets in recessed areas, which can be used for display, storage, or a combination of the two. The first places that always come to mind are the two spaces either side of a chimney breast, usually in living rooms, but sometimes in bedrooms or other rooms, too. Tall and narrow, these recesses can be shelved from floor to ceiling, or boxed in at the bottom to provide cupboards in which to store things out of sight.

Fitted alcoves can be created in all sorts of other areas around the house, too. In the eaves of a top-floor bedroom, for example, or inside a disused fireplace, or at the end of an L-shaped room. Wherever, in fact, you want to put an awkward space to good use. Sometimes, on the other hand, you might wish to run a length of fitted cabinets along an entire wall, creating either dramatic runs of shelving or dynamic combinations of open shelves, closed cupboards, and smaller cubby holes. This type of fitted display area, custom-made to your design, offers instant impact and a striking solution to a host of storage and display problems.

◄◄ (Page 61) Hundreds of
tiny niches provide space for a
wide-ranging selection of
mementoes. Although the
pieces are disparate in nature,
the display works because
they are unified by their size
and confining framework.

► Fitted cupboards either side
of a fireplace are a traditional,
good-looking, and very useful
means of combining both
storage and display.

◄ A glass-fronted cupboard recessed into the wall acts like a picture frame for a selection of personal objects that have been crammed inside.

► This extraordinary glass-and-steel cabinet rises through five storeys of a collectors' house, purpose-built to display a series of fairground figures in the most dramatic way.

Recessed cabinets become part of the framework of a house, so it's best to ensure that they complement the surrounding architecture. Elaborate cornices, skirting board mouldings, and ceiling roses might demand a corresponding attention to detail in the design of a cabinet surround. You may, for example, wish to pick out a detail of the moulding and have it copied, or to emulate the proportions of a fireplace or window frame in the thickness and spacing of your shelving. In a modern home, recesses can be fitted out extremely simply, using inexpensive medium-density fibreboard (MDF) painted the same colour as the walls.

Wood, either painted or unpainted, is the most obvious choice of material for this type of display area, but glass shelving also looks wonderful when run across a recess or alcove. While glass may seem a highly contemporary choice, it's actually so versatile that it can work extremely well in a period property, too. A more unusual effect could be achieved by cladding wooden shelves in a thin veneer of sheet metal, or even by using mirror for the shelves, or using it behind them, or both. Whatever material you choose, never forget the importance of good lighting, which, in a shadowy recess, can make or break a display.

Glass-fronted cabinets

While open cabinets are a wonderful invitation to closely peruse the items on display and perhaps pick them up to examine them, glass-fronted cabinets offer protection against dust and accidental damage, while still allowing a clear view of whatever is inside them. They are the best place in which to display objects that are fragile and easily damaged or very expensive.

Glass-fronted cabinets are also perfect for a kitchen, where they form a barrier against steam, grease, and spills. While much kitchen equipment is not particularly attractive

to look at and therefore best kept behind closed doors, a run of glass will make the room seem more light and airy, and gives you an opportunity to display attractive pieces, whether they're used every day for cooking or eating, or are more ornamental. In bathrooms and conservatories, too, the glass will protect, at least to a certain extent, against humidity. In any case, though, it is inadvisable to display textiles, works on paper, or any other objects that may be damaged by damp, in rooms that suffer from condensation.

Clear glass may seem the obvious choice for this type of display, but bear in mind that there are occasions when

► Corner cabinets are an ideal way to save space while providing both storage and display. This particularly ornate example is showing off simple blue-and-white china.

coloured glass may be equally effective – not necessarily across the entire cabinet, but perhaps in the form of stained-glass panels. And smoked, sandblasted, or etched glass provide alternative options – they will allow a glimpse of what's inside the cabinet while adding an air of mystery.

Wall-hung cabinets

Cabinets that are designed to be hung on walls are often small and fairly unassuming in style, but there's no reason why they shouldn't be grander and more imposing: in oak or mahogany, perhaps with inlays or painted detailing, or even sleek and contemporary, made from glass and stainless steel. Because their shelves are shallow, your display will inevitably be rather linear, though it may be possible, if you wish, to prop up plates or small pictures to offer a decorative background. Think carefully about where to position a wall-

hung cabinet – this is an opportunity to make the most of under-used wall space, or to create a display in a surprising area, while at the same time complementing other furnishings in the room. The height at which it is placed is important, too; eye-level may be the best choice when the pieces on show warrant close inspection. Positioning a wall cabinet higher or lower, on the other hand, can add drama, and emphasizes the versatility of this method of display.

Free-standing cabinets

Adaptable and attractive, free-standing cabinets are probably the most traditional means of displaying any type of item, from the very valuable to the utterly ordinary. And, because by their nature they are portable, they can be placed in almost any position, in any room in the house. Consider the size and scale of the room when choosing a cabinet for

◄ Another corner unit, this one simpler and more contemporary in style, contains a traditional and straightforward collection of plates with a simple pattern.

◄ A combination of plain white crockery and prints, which all have a similar theme and frame, makes for a unified display in this simple, country-style wall cabinet.

◄ This very grand cabinet is the ideal repository for a collection of traditional artefacts, all with a similarly elaborate aesthetic. The painting propped against it on the floor gives the display extra interest.

it – a long, low dining room may require a long, low sideboard; or it may benefit from the addition of a taller piece that draws the eye upward. A tiny sitting room may be swamped by a huge bookcase, but a pair of slightly smaller ones may make the room feel cosy and welcoming.

As pieces of furniture in their own right, free-standing cabinets are generally bought to coordinate with other furnishings. It is harder (though not impossible) to make a display cabinet work well in a room if it contrasts hugely in style with other fixtures and fittings. So, before buying, consider the range of options: purpose-designed display cabinets come in all shapes and sizes. They may be clean-lined and modern, made from simple wood, wood and glass, or brushed stainless steel. They could be in a

◄ Glass-fronted cabinets are ideal display cases, and this one looks splendid filled with an unusual collection of pretty glass and brass knobs. The haphazard way in which they are displayed, and the open door to the cabinet, invite the viewer to pick them up and examine them.

"country" style, perhaps Scandinavian, French, or Shaker, in unadorned wood, or with elaborately painted patterning. They could be Oriental or African, South American or Indian, made from bamboo or lacquer, or decorated with beadwork or mosaic. Or they could be grand and traditional, in a Georgian, Victorian, or "Louis" style, with fine marquetry, inlays, and carving. Department stores and some mail-order catalogues have a good range, and it's worth scouring antique and junk shops for more unusual items. You may even wish to commission one to your own design.

Remember that your choice is not limited to a conventional rectangular cabinet. It could be barrel shaped or arched, pyramidal or even circular, very tall and thin, or short and wide. It could have stable-type double doors, doors

◄ Sometimes even apparently boring objects can be used for a highly interesting display. Here, in a small, wall-hung cabinet, a red backdrop provides a bold setting for rows of padlocks.

► Old-fashioned children's toys and charmingly rustic wooden shelves make for an unusual and appealing contrast to the more contemporary boxy display style.

that hinge horizontally, or no doors at all. It could have rectangular shelving, undulating shelving, or sets of drawers fitted beneath the shelves. It could fit across a corner, or be put on castors and placed anywhere in a room, acting as a dividing screen between two areas, maybe, with the advantage that you will be able to see what's displayed on it from both sides.

It's also worth thinking laterally in order to adapt other types of furniture to a display location – a Chinese chest with the lid left open, perhaps, so that you can look down on a collection of circular vases that are brilliantly glazed inside. A set of aluminium store cabinets might contain, by way of texture and colour contrast, piles of folded saris, while a kitchen dresser could be used in a bathroom. Use traditional

printers' trays (see page 61), or simply add vertical divisions to shelves to create a contemporary "cubby hole" look. Placing identical objects in each hole makes for an impressive, rather formal look, while disparate objects are given a sense of unity by virtue of their consistent framing. You can place small groups within larger cubby holes, or leave some empty for a more airy, spacious feel.

Arranging displays in cabinets

Interior designer Christopher Vane Percy says that creating a display can be rather like mixing and matching in fashion, using patterns, colours, and textures, to create a striking and attractive look. "Try to tell a story," he says. "If you juxtapose objects of different sizes, different materials, and different textures it can be very effective. They may be quite

◄ Thick wooden shelves fitted across the width of a large alcove have a laid-back modern look that is very appealing. The display of books and ornaments has a careful structure but appears quite casual.

► These recesses have been left unshelved so as to hang a selection of prettily patterned china plates. The effect is delightfully fresh and natural.

diverse: a basic rule might be to use a good 'character' piece, something more neutral, and then something made of another material, such as glass or wood."

Because a cabinet or fitted alcove creates the framework for your display, first consider its size, shape, materials, and colours. Large cabinets are best suited either to large pieces or large collections – a few small pieces scattered around will just look silly. In small cabinets, you can afford to spread your pieces out more, as they will have greater individual impact. An unusually shaped cabinet or recess will not suit all types of display; if it tapers toward the

top, for example, it may look odd if all the pieces inside are all the same shape and size, but it could be ideal for collections where some pieces are smaller than others. Where a cabinet or alcove has a very definite shape, a circle or a perfect square, for example, there is something to be said for trying to echo this in the forms of the pieces you display. On the other hand, you could try and find the opposite shape and create a dramatic contrast of form. This is where trial and error comes into play: experiment, move things around, stand back and study them, live with them for a while, and, if necessary, move them again.

The material and colour of a cabinet will also be an influence in setting out a display. A collection of mid-twentieth-century ceramics might look odd in a cabinet made of dark, heavy oak, in this case simple, white-painted surfaces would probably work better. Anything too modern, however, would not be the ideal housing for a set of delicately painted Meissen cups and saucers – their pale colours would be emphasized by a darker background. In fact, the eye will invariably perceive something as being brighter if it's set against a dark background, and vice versa, so painting the inside of a cabinet or alcove is an ideal way of highlighting a display.

Contemporary displays tend toward the minimal rather than the cluttered, so if this is the look you wish to achieve then spread your objects out and allow plenty of space for them to "breathe", looking just as carefully at the shapes between the objects as you do at the objects themselves. Regularity of spacing and repetition of form will create a balance and rhythm that can be highly pleasing. It might be books arranged by height or by the colour of their spines, or it might be a row of vases, each different in shape but approximately the same size. Of course, pieces can be set close together, or even touching, but avoid mixing these two styles of display or it will look like a mistake.

Once you start to overlap pieces, the look becomes less formal, and taken to extremes it results in a wealth of objects of all shapes and sizes crammed close together. This can work very well for a collection that has some sort

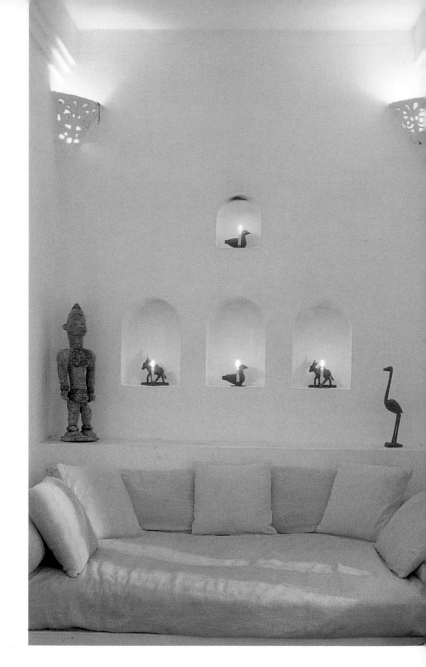

of unity, whether form, colour, or material, but take care to arrange the objects so that they still work together in a display that has balance, flow, and strong visual coherence.

Niches and recesses

The wall niche is the ultimate in display areas – all attention is focused on the object that is placed within it, and its sheer simplicity is the reason for its dramatic potential. Renaissance artists knew this when they designed arched niches for statues and sculptures, and modern architects and interior designers are still aware of it when they punch

◄ Tiny, Moroccan-style niches are the perfect place for a display of small objects. Here, individual candles add flickering, glimmering sparkle.

► Niches of different shapes and sizes create an intriguing pattern in this wall. The bold downlighting in several of them ensures that the objects on display are seen at their absolute best.

◀ The display of blue-and-white china almost merges into the paint-spattered effect background of this shelved recess. Using decorative paint techniques, wallpaper, or tiles, in a recess can help unify and draw attention to the display.

▶ Tucked underneath a series of ascending steps, these intriguing forked sticks lean nonchalantly against the wall. Their strong vertical lines set up a rhythmic dynamism that offsets the horizontal lines elsewhere in the room.

square and rectangular holes in false walls to take high-impact ceramics, glass, and ethnic artifacts.

You can display anything in a niche or recess, from a beautiful designer shoe to a stone carving of a Buddha, a white porcelain vase to an ornate metal candlestick. The two limitations are the quality of the object – its outline, materials, and detailing must be good enough to stand up to the attention it will receive – and its size. Create a calm display by keeping proportions fairly classic, so that the object on display takes up approximately one third to a half of the volume within the niche. This gives the piece room to

"breathe" without it appearing to get lost in the space surrounding it. However, squeezing in an oversized object that only just fits can result in a strong, striking display. Similarly, a tall, thin recess with one object at its base can be equally effective, though do ensure that the width of the object is in proportion to the width of the recess.

Lighting, important in highlighting displays in cabinets, is absolutely vital in niches and recesses. Careful lighting will transform this display area into the focal point of a room, but without good lighting, any object displayed in this way runs the risk of seeming drab and unimportant.

walls & floors

As the largest areas of any room, walls and floors are obvious places on which to mount a display. Far from being limited to the conventional, timid grouping of a few paintings, however, the opportunities with this type of display are enormous, from a few beautiful pieces placed on the floor in a corner to a bold mass of three-dimensional objects across an entire wall.

Walls and floors often provide a large-scale, relatively plain background against which a display of almost any type can really shine. Gorgeous silk robes or textured wool tapestries, embroidered handbags or tufted rugs, hand-thrown ceramic vessels or intricately woven baskets; all will look beautiful against the bare simplicity of a plastered wall or a wooden or stone floor.

Walls and floors as displays in themselves

Walls and floors don't necessarily need objects on them to become a display, of course; sometimes, the pattern, colour, or texture of a wall or floor is wonderful enough for it to need nothing added. Indeed, any other pieces placed on it might not only be lost but also detract from the beautiful expanse of the wall or floor itself.

Take wallpaper, for instance: frequently a byword for a bland and boring background, wallpaper can actually be as eye-catching as a work of art. It could be a modern print, perhaps with pearlized pigments or an optical effect, or it could be a traditional hand-blocked pattern with rich colours or flocking; it could be a fragment of 1960s-style paper pasted onto a section of wall, or a one-off screen-printed paper showing a single, overscaled image; it could even be a digital print taken from one of your own photographs and enlarged in a high-street print shop.

Walls can also be covered in tiles – large, small, or mosaic, arranged in simple blocks of colour or in intricate, Moorish-style patterns; they can be panelled with gloriously grained wood or rendered with rough cement; they can be laminated with metal or plastic sheeting, or be covered with pretty paintwork. There is also scope to paste flat items onto them, such as dried ferns, leaves, or flowers, playing cards, or hand-made paper. With imagination and a little effort, a wall is a blank canvas for displays of amazing invention.

Floors, like walls, can provide a fantastic space for innovative displays. Wooden parquet, for example, laid with patterns of differently coloured blocks of wood, is as intricate and exciting as a work of art; the same can be true of marble, linoleum, vinyl, ceramic tiles, and mosaic. Wall-to wall carpets, while not overly fashionable during recent years, can offer opportunities for unusual treatments, too – many companies will cut and lay carpets with borders or inlaid patterns that are eminently worthy of attention. And there are also more unusual ways of making the most of your floor: laminating a photographic image onto tiles, for example, or placing objects under a glass floor (see page 97), or having a rug custom-woven from a child's drawing. Creating an unexpected display underfoot can be even more exciting than on any shelf, wall, or cabinet.

◄◄ (page 81) The exteriors of buildings can be display areas too. Here, plastic-covered car mirrors, stacked closely in rows, create an unusual and intriguing effect, contrasted against a wall of plain white mosaic tiles.

► Here, rows of pictures, hung across one wall, have been used in a very similar way, demonstrating that this style of display can work just as well in a traditional sitting room as in a more contemporary setting.

◄ The impact of a wall full of pictures is heightened by the fact that they are all the same size, have identical frames, and have been hung at equal distances from each other.

Pictures on walls

Most of us have pictures on our walls – it's a marvellous way to enhance a room and a time-honoured method of display that can cater for any taste and be as costly or affordable as you wish. Traditional oil paintings or watercolours may suit some people, while others may choose black-and white photographs or pen-and-ink sketches, and others may prefer collages or modern abstract works.

Hanging pictures is an art in itself. Strange as it may seem, the hardest thing of all to work with is one single picture, especially a small one. If you can relate it to a nearby three-dimensional object the two can play off each other and start to create a natural display. Pairs of pictures often make more sense, especially when hung symmetrically, perhaps in two recesses either side of a fireplace or on the walls each side of a window. Four pictures, identically framed, can be hung two-up, two-down, while larger numbers of pictures can be either amassed on one wall for a traditional "print room" display, or spaced at regular intervals, their centres all at the same horizontal line (around eye-level), for a more modern look. The further apart your pictures are from each other, the more contemporary the display will appear.

When hanging groups of pictures, it is a good idea to lay them all out on the floor first, standing on a chair to get an idea of how they work together, the aim being to think of them as making up one whole rather than as lots of different elements. Avoid hanging pictures in ascending or descending sizes, take out any whose colours or compositions jar, and have others reframed if necessary.

Choosing mounts and frames that will make pictures look their best often seems a difficult task. In fact, there are conventions that help, although as you become more

◄ An antique African cloth, in muted, earthy tones, has been casually pinned to the wall in a display that provides an attractive contrast to the classic European furniture below.

confident you may wish to break the rules to create unusual effects. Mounts should increase in size according to the size of the picture; extra-large mounts increase the impact and look very modern. White and off-white mounts are subtle and contemporary, while coloured mounts are more decorative and can be used to coordinate with the colours of a room. Frames, too, should increase in size along with the picture, and should, obviously, be sturdy enough to bear the weight of its glass. Frame style is a very personal choice, and may vary according to the style and period of the picture, current fashion, and your interior decoration: an acrylic box will work for a Pop Art print in a loft apartment, while a mahogany or limed-wood frame would suit an oil-on-canvas in a period property, for example. Look for inspiration in art galleries, museums, magazines, and other people's houses, and don't be afraid to ask for advice from an expert framer.

Convention has it that the background colour of a wall should never be more vivid than the brightest colour in a picture hung on it. Working with this theory is safe, certainly, but there may be situations in which works of art demand a highly patterned or very stark background in order to create a truly daring display.

◀ This typically 1950s fabric has been formally framed to give it added weight and significance. Its pattern of squares and curves is echoed in the outlines of the chest of drawers and the accessories placed on it.

▶ Ethnic artifacts displayed in an appropriately ad hoc fashion give this living room a sense of warmth and comfort. The grandly embellished robe hung on the wall is the focal point.

Textile wall hangings

In the Middle Ages, the travelling gentry created entire rooms from wall hangings, which could be folded up and taken from house to house, then hung around walls and over doors as highly effective draught excluders. No longer essential for keeping out the cold, wall hangings are nevertheless still a wonderful means of introducing warmth and colour to a room. While the traditional hunting tapestry will probably look out of place in anything but a large country manor house, there are plenty of other types of wall hanging to choose from: rugs and kilims, quilts and bedspreads, saris, kimonos, felt banners, African kuba cloths, scarves, and shawls, or simply a beautiful length of fabric.

A small textile hanging makes an ideal display when space is restricted, while a series of hangings, or one larger one, will create a huge impact on an expanse of wall. Good places to display them are on the wall behind a sofa, between two symmetrical windows, opposite a dining table, or along a hallway or corridor. They also look fabulous when used in place of a bedhead. Small pieces can be hung informally from a row of hooks, draped over pretty coat hangers, or strung from eyelets pierced in their top two

corners. Robes, or cloth that is hemmed at the top, look fabulous when threaded along a length of cane, while very precious textiles are ideally mounted in a box frame and displayed in the same way as a painting. (See pages 122-5 for practical advice on hanging textiles.)

Three-dimensional objects as wall displays

Collections of identical, or very similar, three-dimensional objects can look amazing when displayed against a wall, either hung from hooks or pegs, or stood on small ledges or brackets. The wall acts as the frame for what becomes a work of art – even if the objects themselves are very ordinary, this treatment elevates them to an iconic status.

This type of display tends to appear more contemporary than traditional, and can lend itself well to kitsch, too. Handbags, for example, are ideal to display against a wall (see page 34), as are items of jewellery, hats, and elaborate evening dresses. Bright colours often work best, particularly against a plain white wall – either a one-colour collection of pieces, or objects that graduate in shade. Alternatively, you could opt for the ultra-minimal look by using white on white, creating a display that is elusive and mysterious.

Whether you hang items in orderly rows, vertical lines, or random arrangements depends on the objects and the style of the room. Oddly, the more kitsch the objects, the better they may look in a formal display, while sophisticated items can be played down with an informal arrangement or given more dignity with a strictly symmetrical grouping.

◀◀ A series of hat moulds hung in rows on the walls of a textile designer's house makes an intriguing three-dimensional alternative to a more conventional row of pictures.

◀ Carefully spaced at regular intervals, a collection of Fornassetti plates picks up on the black colouring used in this kitchen and provides a graphic contrast to the more rustic wood panelling.

▼ A subtle display of creamware plates with fluted edges coordinates with woodwork painted in a delicate shade of green.

Objects displayed on the floor

While shelves, tabletops, mantelpieces, and windowsills provide great places for displays, the floor is the ultimate flat surface, offering the greatest scope of all. Pieces that are simply too large to be placed elsewhere can be put on the floor, in the corners of rooms, next to beds or sofas, or even as a centrepiece, while smaller objects look lovely gathered in intimate areas, such as on a hearth or in a small alcove.

The floor is often the obvious venue for sculptures, which benefit from being positioned so that they can be seen from behind as well as from in front. But you can also pile boxes or baskets of descending size on the floor, or range huge church candlesticks in front of a fireplace. Giant floor cushions can become a display, while pictures can be

▲ An unusual collection of silver-sprayed shoes has been heaped next to a window. Their informality contrasts with the sharp, smart appearance of the floor and glass.

◄ The rough textures of two large woven baskets make a delightful contrast to the smooth surfaces elsewhere in this minimal room.

► A rainbow effect has been created by setting coloured pencils, end to end, into the floor – an innovative alternative to carpet, vinyl or bare floorboards.

propped on the floor in an insouciant fashion rather than being formally attached to a wall. There are no rules as to how you display things on the floor, but simply bear in mind that a contrast in material and texture between the floor and the object on it provides added interest, and that the objects on display will generally be viewed from above, so this viewpoint should offer interest in terms of shape and colour.

Rugs

A rug on the floor is like a picture on the wall: colourful or subtle, bold or intricate in composition, it will provide a point of contrast with plainer surroundings as well as breaking up space or visually anchoring a dining table or bed. Edgar

▶ Walls can become an exciting display in themselves, simply by pressing interesting, attractive flat objects into wet plaster, either in abstract patterns or regular rows.

▶ ▶ Lateral thinking can result in the most dramatic displays. Here, a collection of black-and-white figures stand on the floor beneath rows of gloves pegged to a large noticeboard.

Allen Poe said that "the soul of the apartment is the carpet", and "a judge at common law may be an ordinary man; a good judge of a carpet must be a genius". In other words, choosing floor coverings is not to be undertaken lightly.

And the choice can be rather overwhelming: Aubussons, dhurries, or kilims; Chinese, Turkish, or Indian; woven or tufted, modern or traditional, patterned or plain. Any rug other than the absolute plainest will, however, lift a room and add an extra layer of colour, texture, and composition. Interior designer Christopher Vane Percy said that as soon as you lay a rug on the floor it emphasizes the entire decoration of a room; certain colours jump out and lend themselves to being used elsewhere.

Where to place a rug is often a thorny issue. Try to avoid "floating" it in the middle of an expanse of floor by always overscaling and, says Vane Percy, either place all the main pieces of furniture on it or off it – half measures can look strange. Texture is important, too: a tufted runner looks wonderful in a stone hallway, for example, while delicate silk rugs are marvellous on wooden floorboards.

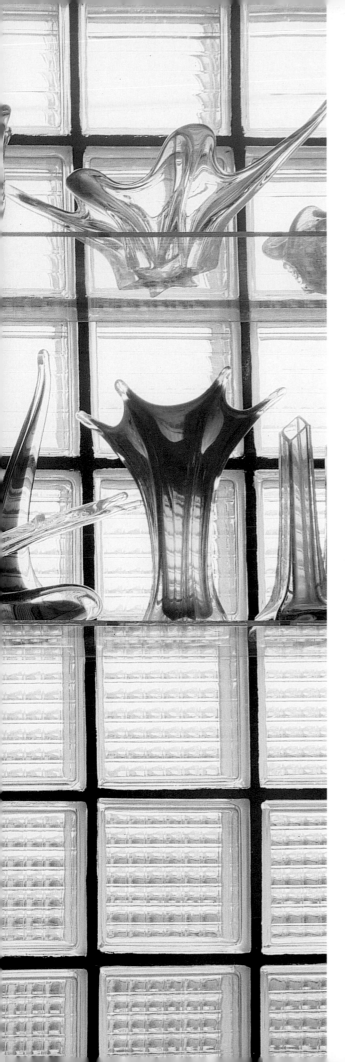

lighting

There's no doubt that good lighting can make the most average of displays look simply stunning, while poor lighting can turn the most superb arrangement of objects into something decidedly dull. Whether your display consists of one huge object or lots of tiny ones, or is placed on a shelf, in a cabinet, on a wall, or on the floor, lighting will breathe life into it, give it character and definition, make it appear more vivid, vigorous, and emphatic, or make it look soft and subtle, gentle and charming, or even elusive, atmospheric, and mysterious. And all at the flick of a switch.

Before deciding on the type of lighting you wish to install, it's important to consider what you want it to achieve. Do you need general or more specific light? Would you prefer it to be soft and diffuse or clear and precise? Do you want a warm yellow light or a crisp white light? Then think about the display you are lighting – its colours and textures, its size and shape, and where it is in the room. Some types of lighting will soften an outline and allow a piece to merge into the background, while others will create harsh lines with dramatic planes of light and dark. Some types will emphasize colour and texture more than others, and some are more appropriate for different locations. Experiment by holding a simple lamp on a long flex at different angles and distances from the display, and see how moving closer or further away affects the shadows, the form, and the clarity of the objects. As when putting together a display, there may be a few straightforward guidelines for lighting, but personal experience and your own imagination are the best guides.

Spotlights

Directional lighting creates the most dramatic effect – think of it as being like a theatre spotlight, with an intense beam, focused on the objects you want to highlight, surrounded by darkness. This type of light emphasizes strong outlines and textures, while casting deep shadows around the display. It can give the effect that the object is floating in a void, and may even be rather surreal.

By lighting just one side or the top or the bottom of an object, its shape will be altered; it may appear to have been cut in half. This works marvellously with the right type of object, but if you find it looks odd you can illuminate the darker side with "fill-in" light from the other direction, and still create a spotlit effect. It is important to consider not only the angle of the light and its intensity, but also the point from which the object or display will be viewed.

Directional light may be composed of uplighters, downlighters, or spotlights in all sorts of shapes and sizes, from floods to mini-spots. Tungsten light, a warm yellow in colour, is fine for this application, and bulbs are available in the form of reflector spotlights. Even better, though, is low-voltage halogen lighting, which gives a crisp, bright, white light with a very direct source. Particularly effective are dichroic reflectors, which take a tiny bulb and focus light in a variety of beam widths. The only drawback is that a transformer is required to reduce the electricity supply to the correct voltage: in the case of downlighters this can usually be hidden in the ceiling.

◄◄ (Page 95) In this picture, lighting becomes a display in itself. An image of multitudes of flowers has been projected onto the wall of a staircase, even over a picture, so that it looks like a shaft of light.

◄ Inset small but powerful uplighters into the floor, adjacent to the skirting, as an unusual method of lighting pictures. This is particularly effective in emphasizing a long, narrow corridor.

Lighting for shelves, cabinets, and alcoves

Displays on shelves or in recesses benefit enormously from some form of artificial lighting – without it the objects may be simply lost in the dark. Your choice of lighting may be simple and straightforward, providing general illumination to bring the display into focus and allow it to be seen, or it could be more dramatic and unusual, adding another level to the effectiveness and impact of your display and creating a focal point in the room.

Before you begin to select specific lights, you will need to decide whether you wish to light the display from above, below, or behind. Downlighting will draw attention to the upper part of the objects, while uplighting concentrates on their bases; backlighting creates silhouettes, so is excellent for concentrating focus on form, but not so good for highlighting colour and texture. Alternatively, you could install several light sources so that the objects are crosslit, which will make them appear vividly three-dimensional.

Often the most straightforward means of lighting shelves and niches is a fluorescent strip, which should be hidden behind a baffle to prevent glare. If you don't like the cool light of fluorescents, tungsten tubes give a softer, warmer light and are dimmable, though rather fragile. A row of small bulbs (again, behind a baffle) would be an alternative, and has the advantage of giving individual illumination to the objects below. Better still is a specific shelf-lighting system, involving miniature, low-voltage lights

◄◄ (Page 109) When an
impressive artwork has been
placed at a focal point, as here,
a row of ceiling lights that lead
toward it serves to heighten
its importance.

◄ A bright downlighter
provides drama to an otherwise
straightforward display of
flowers in a niche. The shelves
to the right have been lit with a
strong side light.

that can be tucked into slimline shelving so the light source is almost invisible, and all you see is the light itself. As with all low-voltage lights, these require a transformer, and you should avoid siting them too near certain types of display as they can become hot. They are available as a track system or a clickstrip, so the tiny bulbs can be placed to complement your display, either at regular intervals or grouped together in clusters.

Low-voltage spots are also excellent as individual downlights or uplights, recessed into the top or the bottom of cabinets or shelves. They are particularly effective when used in conjunction with glass shelves, as their light will dissipate upward or downward through all the objects on display. Use a dichroic reflector bulb to reflect light in a concentrated beam; they come in various widths and wattages, so you can be precise about the effect you create.

Good lighting is essential to the effectiveness of displays in niches and alcoves. The fact that the source of light is invisible gives this single-object display in a large niche an added sense of theatre.

Less usual sources of light for shelves and cabinets include ropelights and fibre-optic lights. In the former, lots of miniature bulbs are set inside a flexible rubber "rope" which can be attached to more or less whatever surface you wish and, of course, even runs around curves. Ropelights are available as mains or low-voltage. Although marvellous for lighting bookshelves in particular, ropelights have one chief disadvantage: when they fail (after about 10,000 hours)

the whole thing has to be replaced. Until recently, fibre-optic lights were used mainly in museums, galleries, and offices. They are an excellent means of lighting a very valuable display, emitting neither ultraviolet rays nor heat. Clean white light is transmitted from a remote source down a bundle of glass fibres to be emitted at the end. Although maintenance is easy, the light source can be bulky, and generally systems are prohibitively expensive.

► The bold shadows of these teapots are caused by a bright midday sun. Placing objects on a window ledge is an effective way of making the most of natural light.

There are also, however, other lighting effects that you can create easily and much more affordably. Using a dimmer switch, for example, can add interest and variety to your display lighting, as can fitting coloured bulbs instead of plain white ones, or even installing coloured filters across the tops of lights. Achieve a touch of retro glamour by shining a light at a rotating glitter ball, which will throw moving splashes of light around a room. Finally, for a touch of romance and magic, why not simply drape pretty white fairylights around and over a display? While they won't provide an efficient overall light, they will add a touch of sparkle and fantasy, which may be all the display requires to bring it to life.

Daylight

When we think of lighting we generally picture an electric light that can be switched on and off at will. But we must not forget that nearly all displays also benefit from natural light. Daylight can provide another wonderful opportunity to experiment with different display effects, especially when objects are positioned near a window. Place a sea shell on a windowsill, for example, and observe how the light changes its appearance through the course of the day, from stark morning light to vivid afternoon light, to soft twilight and the darkness of the evening. Notice also how the effect of the daylight is subject to variations in the weather and the time

◀ Soft daylight falls upon a trio of charming objects. Their muted, gentle colours are enhanced by this unpretentious and natural method of lighting.

▼ Tiny highlights are thrown onto the curvaceous form of this metal sculpture. The natural lighting means they are less harsh than those created by artificial light.

of year. Sometimes the shell will be in shadow, while at others it will appear stark and bright; sometimes it will appear softer and more subtle, while at others it will be precise and clear. Daylight may not be easily controllable, but it is fascinating and surprisingly versatile.

Sometimes, however, daylight can be disadvantageous to a display – the ultraviolet in sunlight can cause textiles, wood, paintings, and works on paper, to fade or deteriorate. If you have precious objects of this sort, it really is worth either displaying them out of range of direct sunlight, rotating them on a regular basis, or using blinds or UV-filters as a protective shield.

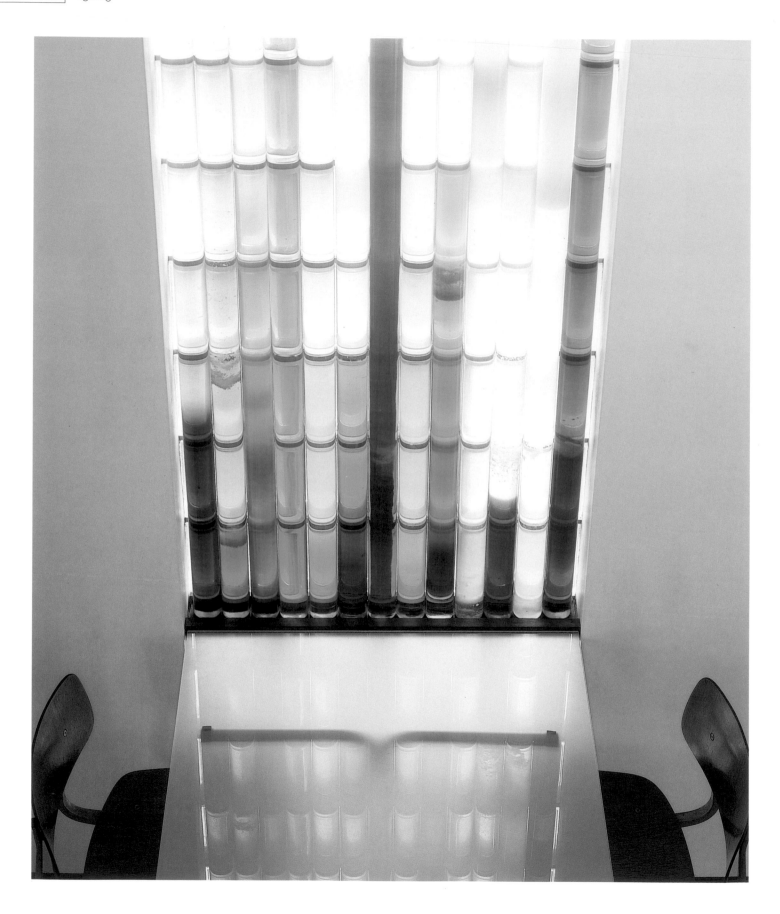

◄ ◄ A modern alternative to the traditional stained-glass window – stacked plastic tubes containing coloured water in a range of toning shades, backlit to give the effect of an illuminated painting.

◄ If you possess objects that create graphic silhouettes, you could arrange them regularly on slim glass shelves and backlight them with a series of fluorescent tubes.

Lighting pictures

If you own a work of art, you'll want to ensure that attention is drawn toward it and also that it is illuminated in a way that complements the decoration of the room as a whole. Before you begin to think about lighting fixtures and fittings, you should give some thought to the picture itself. Its size, colours, framing, and position in the room will all make a substantial difference to the way in which it would be best lit.

Decide whether you would prefer to light it evenly all over, or to focus directional light on just one part of it. You may also need to re-glaze it using non-reflective glass, as light cast on ordinary glass may cause undesirable shadows.

Before the invention of electric light, flickering yellow candlelight was the only means of lighting pictures outside daylight hours, and the pretty gilding of their frames also served to reflect light toward them. Nowadays, we have

◄ A minimal room in a fashionable London hotel is complemented by Philippe Starck lighting. The table is lit from within, making an interesting display of what would otherwise be a rather ordinary piece of furniture.

► Lighting can be a display in itself: this futuristic blue lamp draws the eye at the same time as directing light at the object on display below. The contrast in form and style between the light and the sculpture adds to the display's interest.

many more sophisticated methods at our disposal, but if you have an Old Master-style oil painting in a traditional room you may wish to experiment with candlelight in order to create an air of mystery, intensity, and drama.

On a more contemporary note – and for any picture that requires lighting with evenness and clarity – there are various solutions. One option is to use special picture lights,

set on, above, or below the frame. The longer the arm of the light the better: if it is too short it will throw light onto only a small part of the picture, while the heat from the bulb could cause damage to it. To eliminate reflections and shadows, change the angle of the light until you find the best position.

For greater versatility, choose from ceiling lights, table lamps, floor-standing uplighters, and wall-mounted

downlighters. If you can place a side table near the picture, or preferably one on either side, you may find that a simple lamp with a parchment-coloured shade will be enough, in conjunction with the room's general lighting, to do the trick.

Another option is "Eyeball" lights, recessed in the ceiling near the picture, which can be angled toward it for efficient illumination. The further away they are placed from the picture, the wider and more dispersed the beam of light will be. You will need to experiment with distance to achieve the right width of beam before installing the lights. The same goes for directional lighting on tracks, which may be hung on the ceiling or the walls. Discreet and modern, these can be relatively inexpensive and have the advantage of being easily altered if you decide to move your pictures.

For a very unobtrusive look, use low-voltage halogen uplighters placed on the floor or on an adjacent surface. The fittings are simple and subtle, and the light clear, bright, and excellent at rendering true colours. And to create the most professional effect of all, investigate the possibilities of special fittings with metal louvre-type shutters, which can be hung in a variety of positions and adjusted so that the light thrown on the picture matches its exact dimensions – as if it is glowing all by itself.

Lighting as a display in itself

Of course, light can not only serve to illuminate objects on display, but can also form a focal point of its own. An elaborate French chandelier or an organic 1960s' lamp, for

◄ Plain white boxes provide a useful base for a modern display of simple objects. As they are lit from inside, they also draw the eye to their own spare, uncompromising shape and style.

▲ These unusual, organic, globe-shaped lights on metal poles have been massed in a row. Their contemporary style contrasts subtly with the mask in the background, which has been lit for extra impact.

example, can be treated as a single-object display, as can any source of light that draws attention to its own design, from a dramatic vertical row of paper globes to a series of fluorescent tubes or tungsten lamps in graduating colours. And, lastly, think of being mesmerized by the flickering glow of a real fire, or by romantic, magical candlelight. Delicate tealights, or an assortment of candles in different heights and sizes, create an atmosphere of intimacy and intrigue. Don't stint on numbers, though – the more candles there are, the more effective they will be, while a host of them will create a magnificent display that has no need of further embellishment.

inspirations

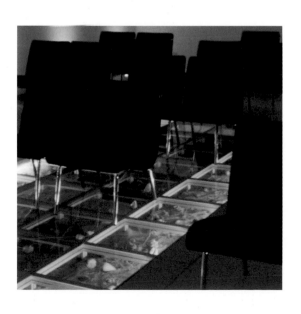

The French novelist and free-thinker Anatole France once said that, "in art, as in love, instinct is enough". And indeed the art of display can rely heavily upon instinct, and upon escaping from the straightforward, the conventional, and sometimes even the tasteful. Displays that have come about as a result of the imagination taking flight are often the most successful, even when the least obvious.

A display may be unusual and innovative simply because of its location: in a lavatory or a home office; on a staircase or a ceiling; high up, low down, or simply in an unexpected corner. It could, equally, be placed at an odd angle, or appear surprisingly casual or dignified in relation to its setting. Perhaps the objects themselves are unusual; anything from Polynesian fish hooks to pebbles, beads to cow bells, soaps to empty picture frames. But if the method of display is truly innovative – the way in which the objects have been hung, mounted, propped, projected, wrapped, lit, or whatever, even though they may be quite ordinary in themselves – the results can be breathtaking, eye-catching, and truly inspirational.

Wrapping, containing, and enclosing

A wide variety of dramatic display effects can be achieved by ignoring conventions or pushing them a stage further than is the norm. If you enjoy wrapping presents, for example, then the perfect method of displaying pretty, inexpensive fabrics is to wrap them around blank books or boxes. (Use a range of sizes, fasten the fabric invisibly in place using double-sided tape, then simply pile them on top of one another.) Or take the Victorian idea of displaying objects inside a glass dome: one piece on show in that way would look desperately old-fashioned, but range twenty pieces in identical domes and it would start to make a statement. Use glass cubes, pillars, or spheres if a different shape would better complement the display. Alternatively, why not put pieces inside test tubes, measuring jugs, or other laboratory or kitchen equipment to create an interesting, if rather hard-edged, effect?

If the idea of unusual containers intrigues you, keep a lookout for receptacles that could be put to good use. Secondhand shops are an excellent source, as are office supply outlets. As well as expensive items, such as salvaged museum display cases, often to be found in architectural antiques centres, and office cabinets, which frequently turn up in junk shops in a variety of styles, materials, and colours, you may come across more affordable but equally desirable containers, such as sewing boxes, tool boxes, filing trays, traditional printers' trays, cutlery trays, flowerpots, magazine holders, egg boxes, or matchboxes. If necessary, paint, line, or cover the container with fabric or paper in a way that best suits your display.

Ingenuity is better than any amount of money when it comes to creating an inspirational display. With a simple laminating machine you can create all sorts of effects: photographs, cards, drawings, or beautiful hand-made papers can be sandwiched between two clear sheets of acrylic and used anywhere you like – on walls, floors, or

ceilings, as kitchen splashbacks, made into lampshades, or propped up as minimal artwork. Cutting-edge florists submerge blooms under water for an intriguing effect; why not take this idea and display objects (waterproof ones, obviously) inside fish tanks or large glass vases for a similar look? Objects that aren't terribly valuable could even be cast inside blocks or spheres of transparent resin – a fairly straightforward process using materials from good craft shops – for a permanent and protective method of display.

Hanging and suspending

There are innumerable ways in which displays can be hung in order to make a dazzling and unusual impression. Achieving this effect can be utterly straightforward, such as simply taking a rug from the floor and hanging it on a wall, like a work of modern art. Both traditional and contemporary designs can look good, particularly if shown against a plain white wall. A more complex display, but one with inimitable style, could be achieved by fitting an acrylic

◄◄ (Page 95) Shell work is a traditional decorative technique. Here, hundreds of white shells have been placed around a large fireplace and mirror. Black paint underneath provides the perfect contrast to show them off.

◄ A thick glass floor makes an impressive surface in this modern office room, especially when underlit with fluorescent blue strip lighting. Beneath is a display of sand and sea shells.

► Strips of reinforced glass make a shiny floor surface in an ultra-modern apartment. The display underneath is lit from below and consists of family mementoes, a traditional idea that contrasts well with the contemporary style above.

shelf below your ceiling and standing objects on it, lit from above. The colours and shapes will make a dramatic impression – a modern version of a fresco painting.

Displays can also be hung across the tops of doorways (but make sure you hang them high enough), or even over the entire doorway in the form of curtains, either beaded or made from a length of gorgeous fabric. Displays can look beautiful in front of windows, where the light will play on them and create fascinating shadows around the room; this is especially wonderful if you hang coloured glass nuggets

or crystals. And, of course, displays can also be hung from ceilings, beams, and archways, or below a shelf, using nylon monofilament (transparent fishing wire) so that their means of suspension is practically invisible. Alternatively, for a more noticeable visual statement, use slim metal chains, ribbons, twisted silk thread, or plaited rope. Or simply use drawing pins to attach papers and fragments of fabric to a wooden door, shutter, or cupboard, or to a cork pinboard.

A little lateral thinking will inevitably result in more ideas on how to hang things: clothes hangers, either

◀ To make a display of net curtains may not seem an obvious concept. With clever lighting, however, they can transform the entire room into a jewel-like enclosure.

▶ A combination of classic framed pictures and empty frames – even a window frame – used as decorative objects in their own right are especially striking displayed against a vividly coloured wall.

wooden or made from pretty padded fabric; pegs, dangling from a string for a rustic, informal look; a row of test tubes wired together and suspended across the width of a wall – the possibilities are limited only by the weight of the objects you are hanging and the practicalities of your space.

Propping, standing, and placing

The easiest way to create a display is to take the object you wish to show off and simply stand it somewhere. But while this may seem obvious, there are plenty of ways in which this method can demonstrate some exciting new ideas. For example, framed paintings, drawings, prints, and the like can be displayed on artists' easels (see page 46), music stands, and lecterns, for a delightfully informal effect. Even more casual would be to prop them up on a chair seat, while in a room where space is at a premium it may be worth investing in a stand on wheels, which can be moved around to suit the occasion. Small, unframed pictures, photographs, and postcards can be placed flat on a coffee table and protected with a sheet of plate glass, tucked into place-card

◄ This large box frame has been specially made to display intricate examples of turned wood in varying combinations. Their graphic lines are pleasantly repetitive.

holders, or displayed on a noticeboard or refrigerator door using smart metal magnets. Textiles may be folded and piled into an open dresser, or rolled so that only their ends are visible, or stretched over artists' stretchers to create the effect of a patterned canvas – simply hang it on the wall.

Coat stands, dummies, mannequins, and busts are all marvellously useful for displaying three-dimensional objects such as clothing, hats, scarves, and jewellery, while shoes can be displayed formally on special stands or informally on the floor or up the stairs.

A wide or little-used staircase, in fact, is an ideal place for displays of items that are repetitive in form but slightly different – they make a great impression when massed in ascending diagonal ranks (see page 57). But to create a really eye-catching display in a truly simple fashion, consider investing in a long, thin lightbox – the kind used by photographers and designers to study transparencies – and use it like a shelf on which to prop any object that would look good when silhouetted by light from below.

Painting, printing, and projecting

A bare wall is a blank canvas for anyone interested in display, but why buy paintings by other people when you can make your own? Those with artistic talent may wish to

◄ A clever and surprising alternative to wallpaper – pressed leaves have been arranged carefully and stuck on to a white wall.

▲ Instead of a conventional headboard, the entire wall behind this bed has been covered with polished wooden objects in repetitive rows of varying shapes and sizes, all suspended in an intricate metal framework.

paint, stamp or stencil directly onto a wall (or even a curtain or a floor) while absolutely anyone can enlarge images or letters on a photocopier and either paste them on or trace around them. The bigger the better if effect is what you are after. Or buy a trio of stretched artists' canvases and paint each in a slightly different shade, using ordinary household emulsion – the result is a triptych with bold but sophisticated appeal. Finally, for an even more avant-garde effect, take an ordinary office slide projector and use it to display an image on a blank wall (see page 95) – for a display with impact that isn't really there.

◄ Why hang art flat against a wall? A row of modern, abstract canvases, all the same size and shape, looks fabulous attached at right angles in an evenly spaced row.

▲ Quilts and other large, flat textiles can be difficult to display. Avoid convention and hang them over a wide A-frame, showing off their colours and patterns to best effect.

practical advice

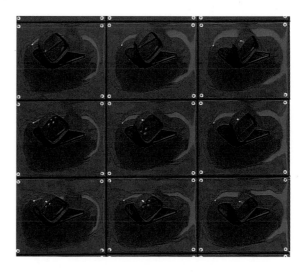

approaches to display

Some practical know how is useful when putting together a display, whether you need to hang a picture or a piece of fabric, put up a shelf, or ensure that a beautiful rug isn't dangerously slippery on a polished floor.

hanging fabric from a batten

Lengths of flat fabric of any type – embroidery, appliqué, painted silk, or simply beautiful fragments of antique printed cloth – can be hung on a wall in such a way that you can't see their support, like a picture but without the frame. The trick is to use a narrow wooden batten and a length of hook-and-loop fastening. Displaying large textiles in this way works particularly effectively in a contemporary room.

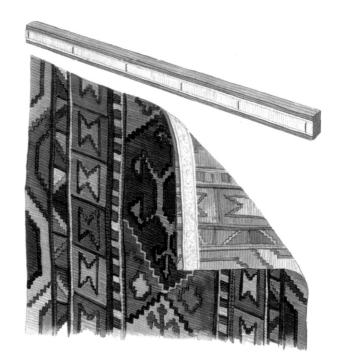

The first step is to assess your fabric. If the fabric is delicate, you will need to sew it onto a backing fabric first. (Remember, however, that you should never cut precious fabric, and you may wish to consult an expert before stitching it.) Cut a piece of medium-weight, pre-washed cotton 2.5cm (1in) larger all round than the display fabric. Turn the edges in, lay the backing fabric hemmed side down on the reverse side of the display fabric, and neatly stitch the edges of the two pieces together.

▲ How heavy is your fabric? Light fabrics will only need one support, but heavier fabrics will need additional battens on each edge. Cut a wooden batten to the same length as the top edge of your fabric (and, if necessary, the bottom and sides). The batten should be as slim as possible – between 1 and 2.5cm (½-1in) thick is ideal. Drill two holes through it and screw it to the wall (see Putting up Shelves in an Alcove, p.127, for more information). Sew one side of a length of hook-and-loop tape along the top edge of the fabric and staple or glue the other side to the batten. Fasten together.

hanging a kimono

Attaching textiles to a wall can be done in a variety of ways, depending on the type of textile, its size, delicacy, and value, and also on the effect you wish to create. Garments, including kimonos, robes, jackets, and coats, are ideally suited to being suspended from a pole, and can create a striking display that will be the focal point of a room.

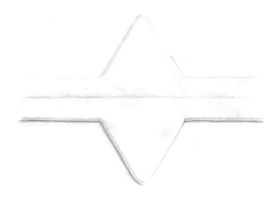

▲ **2** To prevent folds and wrinkles, and to protect the fabric of your garment, you will need to pad the pole with polyester wadding, covered with a fabric that complements the garment in colour and texture (silk works well, or you may prefer a plain cotton). Pre-wash your chosen covering fabric to remove any finishes. Cut a piece of wadding the same length as the pole and wide enough to roll around the pole. If the kimono has an open neck, cut a corresponding shape in the wadding so it will cover this area. Cut the same shape in the covering fabric, but allow 2.5cm (1in) seam allowance all around, plus an extra 2.5cm (1in) at each of the two short ends. Turn over the short ends and machine- or hand-stitch the hems to prevent the edges from fraying.

▲ **1** Lay the kimono on the floor with the sleeves stretched out to each side, and measure its width. Add at least 20cm (8in) extra so the pole will extend beyond the sleeves for hanging. Choose a pole that is strong enough to take the weight of the kimono without sagging, but not so thick that it looks out of proportion. Wood is ideal, but bamboo, metal, or even an acrylic rod could also be used. Carefully cut the pole to length. If using wood, sand the ends for a smooth finish. You may even wish to paint the pole in a colour that complements the kimono or to match your walls.

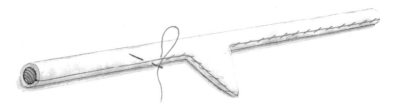

▲ **3** Roll the wadding around the pole and pin the edges together, then stitch. Roll the covering fabric over this and pin then stitch its edges together, using silk or cotton thread in a matching colour. As you sew, tuck the edges inside and use small stitches so that you create an invisible hem. To cover the ends of the wadding, simply tuck the excess covering fabric between the wadding and the pole, if necessary using a tiny stitch or two to hold it in place. Hang the pole from hooks in a corresponding size and complementary material. To attach the hooks you will need to use wall plugs and screws; the hooks should be placed just beyond the ends of the kimono's sleeves, with a short length of pole extending beyond them.

mounting a flat textile on a board

You may wish to display fabric in the same way as a painting, on a backing fabric and board, drawing attention to its intricate detail in an unfussy, modern way. To protect a valuable sample, you could add a box frame with a glass or acrylic cover.

▲ **1** Choose a backing fabric in a colour that complements your textile and that is strong enough to take the weight without sagging. It is advisable to use 100 per cent cotton for valuable textiles, pre-washed to remove any finishes and to allow for shrinkage. Decide how wide you wish the border of the backing fabric to be by laying your textile on top of it. Wide borders look contemporary, but if they're too wide they will draw attention away from the textile. Cut the backing fabric, adding at least 7.5cm (3in) all round. (Allow extra if the board is thick or large.)

▲ **2** Cut a piece of acid-free board to the size of your textile plus its border of backing fabric. Making sure that the grain of the backing fabric is straight, place it on a flat surface, wrong side up, and lay the board on its centre. If you wish, you can add an interlining of very thin wadding to give the textile light padding. Cut this about 5cm (2in) larger than the board on each side and sandwich it between the board and the backing fabric. Cut diagonally across the corners of the wadding and backing fabric as shown above.

▲ **3** Glue around the edges of the board and fold over the interlining, if using, pressing it down smoothly. Allow the glue to dry.

▲ **4** Glue the board again and fold over the backing fabric, smoothing it down. Allow the glue to dry, then neatly hand-stitch the mitred corners together using matching thread. Turn the board over.

▲ **5** To sew the textile onto its mount, first pin it into place, pulling it gently so that it is a little taut, but not stretched. This will prevent it from sagging. Stitch carefully all round, using tiny, regular stitches in a matching colour thread. It may be easier to use a curved needle.

▲ **6** If your textile is very heavy, do not sew along the bottom edge. This will help prevent it sagging. It may also help to sew loose stay lines at intervals across the textile, using matching coloured thread, to support its weight. Display the mounted fabric as it is, or have it box-framed.

mounting a flat textile on a stretcher

If you want to display a large textile (about 40cm/15in square or larger), you will need to attach a wooden stretcher to the backing board to prevent it from warping.

▲ **1** Choose a wooden stretcher that is appropriate for the size of your textile (see step 1 opposite), and cut a piece of backing board to fit. Glue the board securely to the stretcher and leave to dry. Cut the interlining and backing fabric to fit and place the board/stretcher on top of them (see steps 1 and 2 opposite).

▲ **2** Staple the interlining and backing fabric to the stretcher frame, starting at the centres and working towards the corners, pulling the fabric so that the grain is straight as you go. Hand-stitch the mitred corners (see step 4 opposite).

display accessories

Special mounts for three-dimensional objects can be made from acrylic, glass, wood, stone, or metal. They range from the very simple to the more complex, though all are designed to show off the piece on display rather than themselves. Here are some examples.

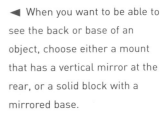

◄ When you want to be able to see the back or base of an object, choose either a mount that has a vertical mirror at the rear, or a solid block with a mirrored base.

► For objects with a rounded or an even, spherical base, rings and solid squares with a cut-out circle are perfect.

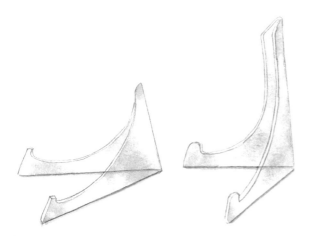

▲ For displaying plates and bowls of a range of sizes, use fixed stands or ones that can be adjusted so the angle of the back rest varies. For hanging plates on walls, you can buy adjustable stands with three or four arms made from clear acrylic. These are preferable to the spring-loaded bracket types, which can damage the objects by exerting undue pressure on them. To prevent scratching, pad the plate on the back with synthetic felt or pre-washed 100 per cent cotton.

◄ A series of small objects can often be displayed to their best advantage in transparent shelving such as this. Depending on the size of your collection, whether it be of shells, tiny teacups, lead soldiers, or whatever, such racks can be used singly, in a pair, or in repetitive rows.

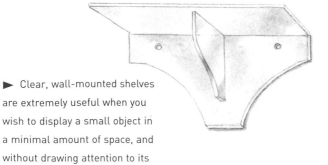

► Clear, wall-mounted shelves are extremely useful when you wish to display a small object in a minimal amount of space, and without drawing attention to its support. They are available in a variety of sizes.

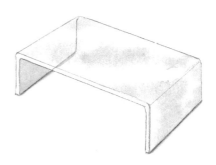

▲ There are a host of versatile, general stands that can be used for displaying all sorts of objects. Stands shaped like an inverted "V", with a lip at the front (left), can be used for small, fairly flat objects, while bridges (right), cubes, and solid "drums" – all available at different heights – are ideal for adding variety to displays of several three-dimensional objects.

putting up shelves in an alcove

The alcoves either side of a chimney breast are an ideal place to fit shelving. The back and walls of the alcove make ready-made supports, and the end result is neat, space-saving and attractive. Putting up shelves, particularly in an alcove, is not difficult, but remember to use a spirit level to check that the shelves are straight from side to side and back to front. Also, as alcoves almost inevitably have slight variations in width and depth from top to bottom, it is best to measure and cut each shelf separately.

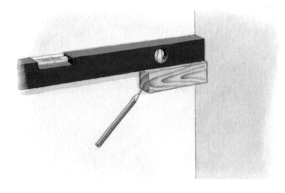

▲ **1** Decide where to place your first shelf and mark the position for its support at the back of one side wall of the alcove, using a spirit level to ensure it is straight.

▲ **2** Using plywood or medium-density fibreboard (MDF), cut a support to the required length and, if possible, cut its front edge at an angle to make it less visible (wear safety goggles and a mask whenever you do any cutting or drilling). Mark the positions for the screws with a bradawl, then drill the holes through the support.

▲ **3** Hold the support to the wall and use a spirit level to check that it is correctly positioned. Mark the position of the drilled holes on the wall by tapping a screw through each of the holes with a hammer. Take the support away and drill holes in the wall at the marked points, the length of your wall plugs plus 3mm (⅛in). The depth of the screw in the wall should be about twice the thickness of the support; 50mm (2in) screws and compatible wall plugs are generally adequate to fix ordinary shelves to a masonry wall. Screw the support tightly to the wall.

▲ 4 Carefully cut a shelf to fit the alcove at this height. Rest the shelf on the support, hold it level, and mark the position for its other support on the opposite wall. Fix the second support as the first. If your alcove is wide, or if you are placing heavy objects on the shelf, you will need to make an additional support for it across the back of the alcove. Rest the shelf on the supports, or glue, nail, or screw it into place. To hide the supports, you can pin and glue a thin plywood panel to the front of the shelves, using 20mm (¾in) panel pins and PVA wood glue.

securing rugs on the floor

Rugs placed straight on a wooden, vinyl, or ceramic floor can often be dangerously slippery, while on fitted carpet they can buckle and wrinkle, which is not only annoying but could cause trips or falls, especially to children, elderly, or infirm people in the house. However, these problems can be avoided invisibly and inexpensively by fitting non-slip matting underneath the rug.

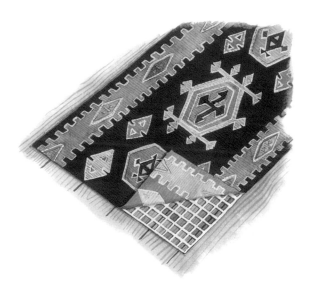

◄ Special non-slip matting is made from either foam or webbing with a low-tack surface. It should be cut to about 5cm (2in) smaller than your rug all round, then laid on a dry, dust-free surface, either hard flooring or carpet. Place or roll the rug into position and press down. The matting should not damage the floor underneath and it is possible to wash some types. Be aware, however, that even when using non-slip matting, you should always replace a rug that is starting to wear, and never put it on a polished surface (you can wax the floor underneath but don't buff it up). And if a rug is placed at the top of the stairs, do ensure that the area is well lit.

making and attaching a box-shaped plinth

A small, wall-hung plinth – or a series of them – in a minimal, boxy style, is an interesting and practical means of displaying small, light objects.

► 1 Wearing safety goggles and a mask, cut six squares of plywood or medium-density fibreboard (MDF). As a general rule, if the largest piece is about 30cm (12in) long, the wood or board should be 20-25mm (¾-1in) thick. However, the square for the front of the box need only be about 6mm (¼in) thick. Drill two holes through one of the thick squares so it can be attached to the wall.

▲ **2** To fit the box together, carefully mark the positions for the screws with a bradawl, then drill the holes. A hole 4.5mm (⅛in) in diameter will be needed to take the shank of a No. 8 wood screw. Then countersink the holes to take the heads of the screws, deep enough so that later you can hide the screw heads by applying filler. Holding one thick piece vertically in a vice, align another thick piece over it, horizontally, and mark the positions for the screws in its edge. Bore pilot holes with either a bradawl or a 3mm (⅛in) drill bit, then drill, to take screws at least 50mm (2in) long. Apply PVA wood glue to both sides, screw together, and wipe off excess glue with a damp cloth. Repeat until you have created a box shape and allow the glue to dry.

▲ **3** Plane the edges of the joints so they are flush with the sides and back of the box. Fill the screw holes with an epoxy filler, allow to dry, and sand the box all over so it is smooth and ready for painting. If you have used plywood, coat the edges with filler and sand them smooth to prevent the laminates showing through the paintwork.

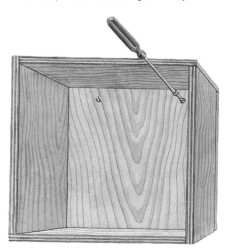

▲ **4** Hold the box to the wall and use a spirit level to check that it is correctly positioned. Mark the position of the two drilled holes on the wall by tapping a screw through each of the holes with a hammer. Take the box away, and drill two holes in the wall at the marked points, the length of your plugs plus 3mm (⅛in). For a brick wall, use compatible wall plugs and screws; for plasterboard, use special plasterboard plugs. The depth of the screw in the wall should be about twice the thickness of your board. Screw the box tightly to the wall.

▲ **5** Pin and glue the thin plywood panel to the front of the box, using 20mm (¾in) panel pins and PVA wood glue. Ensure you wipe off any excess glue with a damp cloth. When the glue has dried, plane or sand the joints flush. Finally paint the plinth, either the same colour as the wall, or in a contrasting shade. Do not use for heavy objects, especially if your wall is made of plasterboard.

making a picture mount

Paper surfaces need a thin cardboard mount to support and protect them. Usually the front of the mount forms a "window" concealing the edges of the picture. If you can't find what you want, it is not too difficult to make your own.

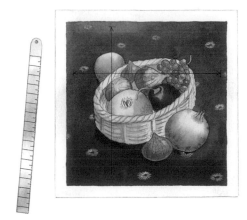

▲ **1** Measure the area of the picture that you wish to see inside the window mount, allowing at least 5mm (⅛in) within the picture on all four sides. Move the picture out of the way. Add about 60mm (2½in) to these measurements all around the picture, plus an extra 5mm (⅛in) at the bottom. This is the size of the outside of your mount. Mark this in pencil on the back of a piece of mounting board, using a set square to ensure that the corners are at right angles. Cut out using a metal rule and craft knife or scalpel with a sharp blade on a cutting surface.

▲ **2** Place the board face down on a clean surface and mark the window dimensions on the back with a pencil and metal ruler. Check the size by placing the picture on top. You can either cut out the window using a scalpel or a professional mount cutter. The latter will give a more attractive angled edge, which smooths the transition between the mount and the picture. When you have cut along the marked lines, the centre of the mount should drop out. You may need to neaten the corners with a sharp scalpel.

▲ **3** Cut another piece of board to the same size as the window mount. Attach the two together with a hinge made from conservation quality materials. Conservators recommend high-quality Japanese paper and home-made starch paste, but acid-free gummed paper provides a suitable alternative.

◄ **4** Paste two short lengths of paper to the back of the picture, at the top. Check the picture's position by placing it in the mount. Once you have decided on its position, attach it to the back of the mount with two more strips of paper, pasted horizontally across the vertical strips, and close the mount.

hanging a picture

How you hang a picture on a wall depends on its weight and size, and also on the type of wall. In some cases, it may only take seconds to do; sometimes, however, a little preparation will be necessary.

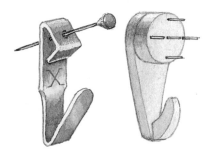

◄ Provided the wall is made of plasterboard or soft plaster, you can simply hammer in either a picture hook-and-nail or a multiple-pin hook.

◄ For a larger picture, use a double- or triple- hook and nail in order to spread the load.

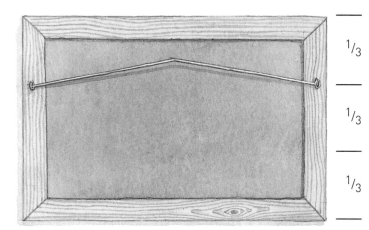

¹/₃

¹/₃

¹/₃

▲ With an awl or drill, make two small holes in the back of the picture frame about a third of the way down from the top and attach screw eyes. Alternatively, and especially if the frame is so narrow that drilling a hole might split the wood, use D-rings attached to the backing board. Stretch a length of cord or twine between the screw eyes or D-rings, doubling it up and knotting tightly. (If the picture frame is heavy, use multi-strand stainless steel wire instead of cord.) Allow a little slack, but not so much that the cord shows above the picture when it is hung. Attaching bumpers of rubber, cork, or plastic to the back of the frame will allow air to circulate behind it.

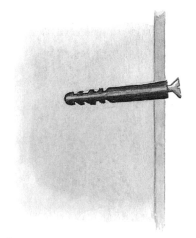

▲ When attaching a picture to a hard wall – brick, cement-and-plaster or concrete – drill a hole and use a wall plug, leaving about 3mm (¹/₈in) of the screw projecting.

► A very large or heavy work is best hung from mirror plates, which allow it to sit flush against the wall. Fix them either at the top edge or on both sides, using brass screws. Concealed mirror plates are neat, but can be tricky to attach to the wall.

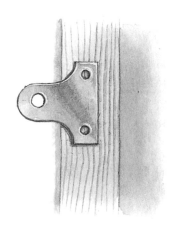

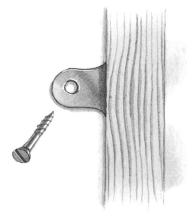

care and preservation

Whether your objects of display are preserved for posterity or irreversibly damaged will depend largely on how you care for them. To avoid damage from corrosion, light exposure, heat, pests, humidity, pollution, and accidental breakages, consider how best to handle, store, and display precious objects. Here are some basic guidelines, but if in doubt, consult a reputable conservation organisation.

Metal objects

The oils and acids from skin can damage metal surfaces; so wear clean cotton gloves to handle metal objects.

Some metals corrode easily in moist conditions, so keep important metal objects at a relative humidity of 55 per cent or lower; 40 per cent in the case of archaeological bronze and iron items. Avoid allowing metal objects to become wet.

Keep metal objects clean and dust-free, but avoid over-polishing or aggressive cleaning, as this will remove the surface of the metal over time. Be particularly careful with

bronze and brass, as it is easy to remove finishes or patinas. Use non-abrasive products and a soft cloth, covering any non-metal areas with plastic. Consult a conservator for advice on cleaning valuable or important pieces.

To prevent silver from tarnishing, place anti-tarnish papers (containing activated carbon) nearby. It is also possible to paint silver (and bronze) with reversible resin or lacquer, although this may eventually turn yellow.

Wooden objects

Exposure to light can cause permanent discolouring of wood, so keep wooden pieces away from direct sunlight, draw curtains, and keep lights off or low when possible. You may wish to apply a UV-filtering film to your windows.

Changes in humidity can cause wood to shrink and crack, and joints to break. High moisture levels can cause mould and infestations. A cool temperature and relative humidity of between 40 and 60 per cent are ideal. It is always a good idea to avoid placing valuable furniture in basements or attics or near working fireplaces. To measure relative humidity, use a hygrometer (available from hardware stores), and to maintain it, use humidifiers and dehumidifiers.

Small holes in wood, or fine dust beneath it, are probably a sign of insect infestation. Prevent this spreading by placing the object in a sealed plastic bag immediately and consult a conservator or extermination expert.

Avoid using oil or silicone polish on wood: the former creates a sticky coating that attracts dirt and darkens the wood, while the latter leaves a film that can interfere with future treatments. On clear-varnished wood recommended treatment is good-quality paste wax, applied in a thin coat no more than once a year. Then simply dust regularly with a soft cloth, removing dirt with a damp cloth if necessary. If the wood is lacquered, painted, or gilded, it can probably be dusted lightly with a soft, natural bristle brush, but it is always advisable to consult an expert first.

Books

Protect rare and valuable books from ultraviolet light (which can cause deterioration and fading) by keeping lights off or low as often as possible, and/or blocking light with curtains or UV-filtering film. Extreme temperatures are also damaging, so keep books away from radiators, fires, and outside walls.

Stand books on shelves vertically, not too tightly packed, and with support from other books or from bookends. Place large books horizontally, in piles of no more than two or three; with squares of felt between them if necessary. Allow air to circulate around the back of the shelf. If you notice signs of pests, consult a conservator immediately.

Books can attract a great deal of dust: clean regularly with a cloth, soft brush, or vacuum cleaner with the suction reduced and a sheer cloth over the nozzle. If a valuable book is damaged, do not try to repair it yourself, but consult a professional book binder or a book conservator.

Ceramics and glassware

When moving a ceramic or glass object, pick it up by its body rather than a handle, rim, or spout, and clear a space to put it down before moving it. It may be safer to use a padded box, particularly if you are going up or down stairs. Put padding between items in the box, too.

Ceramic and glass items should be kept free from dust and grease, ideally protected under glass. If you need to clean them, use a soft, clean white cloth, a soft brush, or a damp cloth; avoid household cleaners. When washing very fragile ceramic or glass objects in a sink, line it first with soft cloths. (Do not, however, wash unglazed earthenware, or ceramic or glass pieces that have been painted or repaired.) If bone china has been stained – perhaps by tea or coffee – soak it in biological washing powder. Consult a conservator before attempting to clean an important piece.

Ceramics can crack or their glaze be damaged by very high or low temperatures or sudden changes of temperature. In very humid conditions mould can grow, which may stain.

Do not leave liquid standing inside a glass vessel for a long period – it will etch the surface of the glass and leave it with a cloudy appearance that cannot be altered.

If possible, display ceramics and glass on solid, level, flat surfaces, away from pets, small children, and high-traffic areas . There are various ways to fix fragile, unsteady objects to a flat surface. If the object is of little value, use double-sided sticky tape, adhesive hook-and-loop strips, or certain types of putty. Much better for valuable pieces is microcrystalline wax ("museum wax"), which comes in a solid block and must be melted. Make small dots of wax on the base of the object and place it in position; the wax will solidify and hold it in place. You can pour a little clean, dry sand into a non-transparent, top-heavy object to weight it.

Carpets and rugs

Always vacuum rugs underneath as well as on top, to remove grit from between the knots. Sewing a strip of cotton tape to the edges of a rug will help strengthen it and prevent fraying.

If you spill red wine on a carpet, sponge with white wine immediately, then rinse with warm water. If necessary, sponge with borax solution, or cover the stain with salt to absorb the wine, then dab gently with hot water. If the fabric is not washable, use upholstery shampoo and sprinkle on talcum powder, leave for an hour, then sponge and blot dry.

Other textiles

Light can cause fabric to fade, and finishes (such as starch) to turn yellow. Try to display textiles in low light, and rotate them if possible. Do not store or display textiles near direct sources of heat, and maintain relative humidity at between 35 and 70 per cent to avoid excess drying or mould growth.

Dust, grit, and insect infestation will all cause damage, so gently vacuum sturdy textiles on a regular basis, or use a soft brush to dust into the nozzle of the vacuum cleaner. Use a sheer fabric mesh over the nozzle to catch any loose fibres.

Consult a conservator for advice on maintaining fragile textiles, as they will need special treatment. Wear cotton gloves to handle delicate fabrics, and first remove jewellery, belts, and so on, which might catch.

Paintings

To protect against environmental damage, dust and debris, and accidents when handling, screw an archival cardboard backing to the back of a painting. It should cover the whole of the painting and be attached to the reverse of the stretcher; ask a reputable framer or conservator to do this for you.

Avoid large fluctuations of temperature or humidity in a room where you have a valuable painting – a relative humidity of between 40 and 60 percent and a temperature of 20°C (68°F) is best. If possible, avoid hanging valuable pictures on outside walls, but if you do wish to do so, place rubber spacers on the back of the frame to allow air to circulate. Avoid hanging valuable pictures over working fireplaces, radiators, heating, or air circulation vents, too.

Light can be very damaging to paintings; ideally, hang them out of direct sunlight, or use UV-filters on windows and lights. Picture lights may heat paintings unevenly and damage them – recessed or ceiling-mounted spotlights are better. Halogen bulbs emit a high level of ultraviolet, so it is advisable either to fit a UV-filter or use tungsten bulbs.

Dust paintings every four to six months, using a soft, white-bristle brush. If you notice any loose, cracked, or flaking paint, tears in the canvas, mould, or insect infestation, consult a professional restorer or conservator.

Works of art on paper

The best way to protect a work on paper is to frame it properly, using a mount and backboard made from non-acidic materials (100 per cent ragboard, conservation board, museum board, or acid-free board), glass or rigid acrylic (preferably with a UV-filter), and a well-sealed frame. (Do not use acrylic with pastels, charcoal, or chalk, as it has a static charge which can damage such works.) To attach the work to the backboard, use either photo corners made from archival paper or hinges attached to upper corners. Hinges should be made from Japanese paper and stuck with starch paste, or from acid-free gummed paper tape. Never use spray mount, sticky tape, or standard glues. Do not allow the glass or acrylic to touch the work. The gap between the backboard and the frame should be sealed with gummed paper tape, which allows the work to breathe.

Unframed works on paper can be kept in large folders made of conservation board and stored flat in boxes (preferably metal rather than wood, which emits acidic gases). Separate them with a flat layer of acid-free tissue and handle wearing clean, white cotton gloves.

To prevent works on paper from drying out or becoming mouldy, maintain humidity at between 40 and 60 per cent and aim for a temperature of between 15 and 21°C (60-70°F), using air conditioning, fans, humidifiers, and dehumidifiers. If you notice foxing (mottled brown spots caused by mould), rusting, or flaking on a work, unframe it and air it immediately. In severe cases, you should also seek advice from a conservator. Never hang a valuable piece over a working fireplace, in direct sunlight, or on an exterior wall. Avoid storing works on paper in attics or basements.

Light, particularly ultraviolet light, can cause works on paper to fade, darken, or become brittle. Ideally, valuable works should be rotated and hung in an area with as little exposure to daylight, halogen, and fluorescent light as possible. Use UV-filters or tungsten lighting; but as the latter gives off heat, don't site the picture to close to it.

Insurance and security

Most household insurance policies will not cover items or collections of very high value, so always check your policy and, if you find that certain valuable items are not covered, discuss your needs with your insurer. You may need to take out separate cover with a specialist insurer.

Take clear, close-up photographs of pieces, including any labels, markings, or damage and showing a scale, label them clearly, and store them in a safe place. In addition, keep any relevant records and receipts, to help recover them if they are stolen and also to facilitate any insurance claim.

If you possess valuable collections or works of art, a basic security measure would be to fit high-standard door and window locks, making a potential thief's task more time-consuming, more difficult, and, therefore, more off-putting. Fit mortice locks on doors, with key-operated bolts at the top and bottom of back and side doors, and key-operated locks on ground-floor windows and accessible upstairs windows. Motion-activated external lights, internal timer lights, gravel paths, and thorny bushes under windows are also good ways to deter potential burglars.

The more valuable, transportable, or readily disposable a building's contents are, the more extensive its physical protection needs to be. If you have any very valuable objects, you may also wish to consider a professionally designed, installed, maintained, and monitored intruder alarm system linked to an approved alarm monitoring centre. This may also be used with an automatic fire detection system, which will link up with the local fire service.

If your valuables are kept within one room, you can improve its security with a reinforced door, lockable metal window shutters and/or security cameras. Consult a police crime prevention officer or reputable security firm for advice.

It is also possible to mark individual items with invisible, micro-sized dots. These codes are stored on a police database and can be used to identify stolen goods. This may help you recover your property in the event of a theft and may also act as a deterrent, if you advertize the fact that your possessions are security-marked using small stickers on your windows.

directory

Ready-made shelving and cabinets

ABC Carpet & Home
881 & 888 Broadway at E. 19th Street
New York NY 10003
USA
Tel: +1 212 473 3000
and
777 South Congress
(between Linton & Atlantic on I-95)
Delray Beach
Florida
USA
Tel: +1 561 279 7777
www.abchome.com

Aero
347–349 Kings Road
London SW3 5ES
UK
Tel: +44 (0)20 7351 0511
Fax: +44 (0)20 7351 0522
www.aeroliving.com

Alias
Via dei Videtti 2
24064 Grumello del Monte
Bergamo
Italy
Tel: +39 035 44 22 511
www.aliasdesign.it

Aram
110 Drury Lane
London WC2B 5SG
UK
Tel: +44 (0)20 7557 7557
Fax: +44 (0)20 7557 7558

Atrium
22–24 St Giles High Street
London WC2H 8TA
UK
Tel: +44 (0)20 7379 7288
www.atrium.ltd.uk

B&B Italia
150 East 58th Street
New York NY 10155
USA
Tel: +1 800 872 1697
www.bebitalia.it

The Bachelor Pad
36 St Stephen Street
Edinburgh EH3 5AL
UK
Tel: +44 (0)131 226 6355
www.thebachelorpad.org

Blu Dot Design & Manufacturing Inc
3306 5th Street NE
Minneapolis MN55418
USA
Tel: +1 612 782 1844
www.bludot.com

Bo Concept
158 Tottenham Court Road
London W1 7NH
UK
Tel: +44 (0)1202 317 317
www.boconcept.co.uk

Charles Page Furniture and Interior Design
61 Fairfax Road
London NW6 4EE
UK
Tel: +44 (0)20 7328 9851
Fax: +44 (0)20 7328 7240

The Conran Shop
Michelin House
81 Fulham Road
London SW3 6RD
UK
Tel: +44 (0)20 7589 7401
Fax: +44 (0)20 7823 7015

The Conran Shop
117 rue du Bac
75007 Paris
France
Tel: +33 1 42 84 10 01
Fax: +33 1 42 84 29 75
and
30 boulevard des Capucines
75009 Paris
France
Tel: +33 1 53 43 29 00
Fax: +33 1 53 43 29 39
www.conran.com

The Terence Conran Shop
Bridgemarket
407 East 59th Street
New York NY 10022
USA
Tel: +1 212 755 9079
Fax: +1 212 888 3008
www.conran.com

The Cotswold Company
Tel: +44 (0)870 600 3436 for mail order
www.cotswoldco.com

ddc domus design collection
181 Madison Avenue
New York NY 10016
USA
Tel: +1 212 685 0800
www.ddcnyc.com

Design Center of the Americas
1855 Griffin Road
Suite A282
Dania Beach
Florida 33004
USA
Tel: +1 954 920 7997
www.dcota.com

EmmeBi
Via C Monteverdi 28
20031 Cesano Maderno
Milan
Italy
Tel: +39 0362 502 296
www.emmebidesign.com

Former
Via per Cantu 43
22060 Montesolaro di Carimate (Co)
Italy
Tel: +39 031 780 252
www.former.it

Geoffrey Drayton
85 Hampstead Road
London NW1 2PL
UK
Tel: +44 (0)20 7387 5840
www.geoffrey-drayton.co.uk

Habitat UK
Tel: +44 (0)845 601 0740 for UK branches
www.habitat.net

Habitat
8 rue de Pont Neuf
75001 Paris
France
Tel: +33 1 53 00 99 88
www.habitat.net (for French branches)

Heal's
196 Tottenham Court Road
London W1T 7LQ
UK
Tel: +44 (0)20 7636 1666

The Holding Company
241–245 Kings Road
London SW3 5EL
UK
Tel: +44 (0)20 7352 1600
www.theholdingcompany.co.uk

IKEA
Barkarby, Box 903
175 29 Järfälla
Stockholm
Sweden
and branches
Tel: + 46 8 795 40 00
www.ikea.com (for branches)

Ligne Roset
Tel: +44 (0)845 602 0267 for UK stockists
www.ligne-roset.co.uk

Maxalto
Strada Provinciale 32
22060 Novedrate (Co)
Italy
Tel: +39 031 795 213

MDF Italia
Via Morimondo 5/7
20143 Milan
Italy
Tel: +39 0281 804 100
www.mdfitalia.it

Molteni & C
Via Rossini 50
20034 Giussano
Milan
Italy
Tel: +39 0362 3591
www.molteni.it

Morgan River
St Jude's Church
Dulwich Road
London SE24 0PB
UK
Tel: +44 (0)20 7737 1371
Fax: +44 (0)20 7274 2023

Noel Hennessy
6 Cavendish Square
London W1M 9HA
UK
Tel: +44 (0)20 7323 3360
Fax: +44 (0)20 7323 3361
www.noelhennessy.com

Pavilion Rattan
Unit 4, Mill 2
Pleasley Vale Business Park (off Outgang Lane)
Pleasley
Derby NG19 8RL
UK
Tel: +44 (0)1623 811343
Fax: +44 (0)1623 810123
www.pavilionrattan.co.uk

Pilma
Avinguda Diagonal 403
08008 Barcelona
Spain
Tel: +34 93 416 13 99
Fax: +34 93 217 90 77
www.pilma.com

Porro
Via per Cantu 35
22060 Montesolaro (Co)
Italy
Tel: +39 031 78 02 37
www.porro.com

Pottery Barn
Tel: +1 800 922 5507 for branches
www.potterybarn.com

proctor:rihl
63 Cross Street
London N1 2BB
UK
Tel: +44 (0)20 7704 6003
Fax: +44 (0)20 7688 0478

Purves & Purves
220–224 Tottenham Court Road
London W1T 7PZ
UK
Tel: +44 (0)20 7580 8223
Fax: +44 (0)20 7580 8244

Roche Bobois
14–18 rue de Lyon
75012 Paris
France
and branches
Tel: +33 1 53 46 10 20 for French branches
www.roche-bobois.com

R.O.O.M.
Alströmergatan 20 (Box 49024)
100 28 Stockholm
Sweden
Tel: + 46 8 692 50 00
and
Ris Skolevei 1 (Vinderen)
(Postboks 87)
0319 Oslo
Norway
Tel: +47 22 13 64 00

Room by Wellis
Ettiswilerstrasse 24
CH-6130 Willisau
Switzerland
Tel: +41 041 9 725 725
www.roombywellis.com

Schneller Wohnen
Pohlstrasse 58
Tiergarten
Berlin
Germany
Tel: +49 30 262 7081

SCP
135–139 Curtain Road
London, EC2A 3BX
UK
Tel: +44 (0)20 7739 1869
www.scp.co.uk

Stone Circle
Tor House
45 Chapel Lane Crich
Matlock
UK
Derbyshire DE4 5BU
Tel: +44 (0)1773 850081
www.stonecircle.co.uk

STUA
Poligono 26
E 20115 Astigarraga
San Sebastian
Spain
Tel: +34 943 330 188
Fax: +34 943 556 002
www.stua.com

System 180
387 King Street
London W6 9NJ
UK
Tel: +44 (0)20 8748 6200
www.system180.co.uk

TK33
Schiessestädtstrasse 18
Theresienhöhe
80339 Munich
Germany
Tel: +49 895 407 433 0
www.tk33.de

Universal Providers
86 Golborne Road
London W10 5PS
UK
Tel: +44 (0)20 8960 3736

Valentini mobili s.r.l.
Via Garibaldi 17
25081 Bedizzole (BS)
Italy
Tel: +39 030 687 0773
Fax: +39 030 687 0199

Viaduct
1–10 Summer's Street
London EC1R 5BD
UK
Tel: +44 (0)20 7278 8456
Fax: +44 (0)20 7278 2844

Vinçon
Passeig de Gracia 96
08008 Barcelona
Spain
Tel: +34 93 215 60 50
Fax: +34 93 215 50 37
and
Castello 18
28001 Madrid
Spain
Tel: +34 91 578 05 20
Fax: +34 91 431 16 11
www.vincon.com

Specialist display furniture

Dauphin Museum Services Ltd
PO Box 602
East Oxford OX44 9LU
UK
Tel: +44 (0)1865 343542
Fax: +44 (0)1865 343307

Morton Booth Co
PO Box 123
Joplin
MO 64802
USA
Tel: +1 800 543 5390
www.mortonbooth.com

Quadrant 4
Shakenhurst
Cleobury Mortimer
Kidderminster DY14 9AR
UK
Tel: +44 (0)1299 832300
Fax: +44 (0)1299 832676

Rapid Racking
Kemble Business Park
Kemble
Cirencester
Gloucester GL7 6BQ
UK
Tel: +44 (0)1285 686868
Fax: +44 (0)1285 686968
www.rapid-racking.co.uk

Shopkit Designs Ltd
100 Cecil Street
North Watford
Herts WD2 5AD
UK
Tel: +44 (0)1923 818282
Fax: +44 (0)1923 818280
www.shopkit.com

D&J Simons & Sons Ltd
122–150 Hackney Road
London E2 7QS
UK
Tel: +44 (0)20 7739 3744
Fax: +44 (0)20 7739 4452/2984/1694
email: dsimons@djsimons.co.uk

HC Slingsby Plc
Preston Street
Bradford BD7 1JF
UK
Tel: +44 (0)1274 721591 for branches
Fax: +44 (0)1274 723044

Stephenson Blake
199 Upper Allen Street
Sheffield S3 7GW
UK
Tel: +44 (0)114 272 8325
Fax: +44 (0)114 272 0065
www.stephensonblake.co.uk

Stringer
151–161 Tunnel Avenue
Greenwich Peninsula
London SE10 0PW
UK
Tel: +44 (0)20 8293 4242
Fax: +44 (0)20 8293 4368

Vitsoe Ltd
85 Arlington Avenue
London N1 7BA
UK
Tel: +44 (0)20 7354 8444
Fax: +44 (0)20 7354 9888
www.vitsoe.com

Willow Glen Kitchen & Bath
351 Willow Street
San Jose CA 95110
USA
Tel: +1 408 293 2284
Fax: +1 408 293 9476
www.willowglen.com

Wood Bros (Furniture)
London Road, Ware
Herts SG12 9QH
UK
Tel: +44 (0)1920 469241
Fax: +44 (0)1920 464388

The Worden Company
199 East 17th Street
Holland
Michigan 49423
USA
Tel: +1 800 748 0561
www.wordencompany.com

Lighting

Absolute Action
Focus House
6 Tonbridge Road, Maidstone
Kent ME16 8RP
UK
Tel: +44 (0)1622 351000
Fax: +44 (0)1622 351001
www.absolute-action.com

Aktiva Systems
10b Spring Place
London NW5 3BH
UK
Tel: +44 (0)20 7428 9325

Artemide
Via Bergamo 18
20010 Pregnana Milanese
(Mi) Italia
Casella Postale nr. 9
Italy
Tel: +39 02 93518181
Fax +39 02 93590254/93590496
email: info@artemide.com
or Tel: +39 800 834093 for branches and information
www.artemide.com

Artemide
106 Great Russell Street
London WC1B 3NB
UK
Tel: +44 (0)20 7631 5200
Fax: +44 (0)20 7631 5222
www.artemide.com

Bruck Lighting Systems
Costa Mesa
CA 92626
USA
Tel: +1 714 424 0500
www.brucklighting.com

Chelsea Lighting Design
Unit 1, 23a Smith Street
London SW3 4EJ
UK
Tel: +44 (0)20 7824 8144
Fax: +44 (0)20 7823 4812

Christopher Wray
591–593 Kings Road
London SW6 2YW
UK
Tel: +44 (0)20 7751 8701
www.christopherwray.com

Concord: marlin
The Lighting Centre
14 Warren Street
London W1T 5LL
UK
Tel: +44 (0)20 7380 3670
and
Avis Way
Newhaven
East Sussex RN9 0ED
UK
Tel: +44 (0)1273 515811
Fax: +44 (0)1273 512688

Cube L.I.D
Units 1–2
66 Western Road
Tring
Herts HP23 4BB
UK
Tel: +44 (0)1442 823363
Fax: +44 (0)1442 823656

Erco Lighting Ltd
38 Dover Street
London W1S 4NL
UK
Tel: +44 (0)20 7408 0320
www.erco.com

Helvar
Hawley Mill
Hawley Road
Dartford
Kent DA2 7SY
UK
Tel: +44 (0)1322 222211
www.helvar.co.uk

Hessamerica
PO Box 430
Shelby
North Carolina 28151
USA
Tel: +1 704 471 2211

iGuzzini
ss 77, km 102
62019 Recanati – MC
Italy
Tel: +39 071 758 81
www.iguzzini.it

John Cullen Lighting
585 Kings Road
London SW6 2EH
UK
Tel: +44 (0)20 7371 5400
Fax: +44 (0)20 7371 7799
www.johncullenlighting.co.uk

John Lewis
Tel: +44 (0)20 7629 7711 for UK branches
www.johnlewis.com

Lighting Design
14 Boucher Way
Boucher Crescent
Belfast BT12 6RE
UK
Tel: +44 (0)28 9066 6878
Fax: +44 (0)28 9066 6857

Light Projects
23 Jacob Street
London SE1 2BG
UK
Tel: +44 (0)20 7231 8282
Fax: +44 (0)20 7237 4342

London Lighting Co
135 Fulham Road
London SW3 6RT
UK
Tel: +44 (0)20 7589 3612
Fax: +44 (0)20 7581 9652

Louis Poulsen Lighting Inc
3260 Meridan Parkway
Fort Lauderdale FL 33331
USA
Tel: +1 954 349 2525
www.louispoulsen.com

Mr Resistor
21 Lydden Road
Wandsworth
London SW18 4LT
UK
Tel: +44 (0)20 8874 2234
Fax: +44 (0)20 8871 2262
www.mr-resistor.co.uk

Peter Burian Associates
Hillview
Vale of Health
London NW3 1AN
UK
Tel: +44 (0)20 7431 2345
Fax: +44 (0)20 7435 2294

Sirmos
30–00 47th Avenue
Long Island City
New York NY 11101
USA
Tel: +1 718 786 5920

Conservation organisations

Many of the organisations listed below will suggest
a suitable conservator or restorer.

**The American Institute for Conservation of Historic
and Artistic Works**
1717 K Street NW, Suite 200
Washington DC 20006
USA
Tel: +1 202 452 9545
Fax: +1 202 452 9328
www.aic.stanford.edu

Canadian Association of Professional Conservators
c/o Canadian Museums Association
280 Metcalfe Street, Suite 400
Ottawa
Ontario K2P 1R7
Canada
Tel: +1 613 567 0099
Fax: +1 613 233 5438

**European Confederation of Conservator-Restorers'
Organizations**
Coberg 70
1000 Brussels
Belgium
Tel: +32 2 230 7291

Institut Français de Restauration
150 avenue President Wilson
93210 La Plaine St Denis
France
Tel: +33 1 49 46 57 00

United Kingdom Institute for Conservation
109 The Chandlery
50 Westminster Bridge Road
London SE1 7QY
UK
Tel: +44 (0)20 7721 8721
Fax: +44 (0)20 7721 8722

Conservation suppliers

Carr McLean
461 Horner Avenue
Toronto
Ontario M8W 4X2
Canada
Tel: +1 416 252 3371
Fax: +1 416 252 9203
email: cmclean@carrmclean.ca
www.carrmclean.ca

Conservation by Design
5 Singer Way
Woburn Road Industrial Estate
Kempston
Beds MK42 7AW
UK
Tel: +44 (0)1234 853555
Fax: +44 (0)1234 852334
www.conservation-by-design.co.uk

Conservator's Emporium
1805 Standing Rock Circle
Reno
NV 89511
USA
Tel: +1 775 852 0404
Fax: +1 775 852 3737
www.consemp.com

Long Life for Art
Christoph Waller
Im Bueckle 4
D–79288 Gottenheim
Germany
Tel: +49 766 594 0390
Fax: +49 766 594 0391
www.cwaller.de

Picreator Enterprises
44 Park View Gardens
London NW4 2PN
UK
Tel: +44 (0)20 8202 8972
Fax: +44 (0)20 8202 3435

G Ryder & Co
Denbigh Road
Bletchley
Milton Keynes
Bucks MK1 1DG
UK
Tel: +44 (0)1908 375524
Fax: +44 (0)1908 373658

Talas
568 Broadway
New York NY 10012
USA
Tel: +1 212 219 0770
Fax: +1 212 219 0735
www.talasonline.com

The Textile Restoration Studio
2 Talbot Road
Bowdon
Altrincham
Cheshire WA14 3JD
UK
Tel/Fax: +44 (0)161 928 0020

Security advice

The British Security Industry Association (BSIA)
Security House
Barbourne Road
Worcester WR1 1RS
UK
Tel: +44 (0)1905 21464
Fax: +44 (0)1905 613625
www.bsia.co.uk

index

Page numbers in *italic* refer to the illustrations

bibliography

The Art of Seeing, Paul Zelanski and Mary Pat Fisher, Prentice-Hall (1999)

At Home with Art, Estelle Ellis, Caroline Seebohm and Christopher Simon Sykes, Thames & Hudson (1999)

Collecting & Display, Alistair McAlpine and Cathy Giangrande, Conran Octopus (1998)

Collins Complete DIY Manual, Albert Jackson and David Day, HarperCollins (2001)

The Complete DIY Manual, Mike Lawrence, Lorenz Books (1999)

David Hicks on Decoration, David Hicks, Britwell Books (1972)

David Hicks on Decoration, David Hicks, Frewin (1966)

The Decoration of Houses, Edith Wharton and Ogden Codman Jr, W.W. Norton & Co (1996)

Easy Living, Terence Conran, Conran Octopus (1999)

Get the Look, Rebecca Tanqueray, Kyle Cathie (2000)

Kevin McCloud's Lighting Book, Kevin McCloud, Ebury Press (1999)

Living with Art, Karen Wheeler, Carlton Books (2000)

Living with Books, Alan Powers, Mitchell Beazley (1999)

Recipes and Ideas: Lighting, Sally Storey, Quadrille (2000)

Windows: the Art of Retail Display, Mary Portas, Thames & Hudson (1999)

acknowledgments

Mitchell Beazley would like to acknowledge and thank the following for providing images for use in this book.

Front cover Ray Main/Mainstream
Back cover Ray Main/Mainstream/designer Ian Manking

Key: a above, b below, l left, r right

2, 6–7 Deidi Von Schaewen; 8 Interior Archive/Andrew Wood/designer: Leonie Lee Whittle/Snap Dragon; 9 Narratives; 10 Marie Claire Maison/Gilles de Chabaneix/stylist: Marion Bayle; 11a Red Cover/Brian Harrison; 11b Abode; 12l Narratives/Jan Baldwin; 12r Marie Claire Maison/Nicolas Tosi/stylist: Catherine Ardouin; 13 Andreas Von Einsiedel; 14–15, 15r, 16 Ray Main/Mainstream; 17 View/Chris Gascoigne; 19 Andreas von Einsiedel; 20 Interior Archive/Nicolas Bruant/designer: Carolyn Quartermaine; 21, 22 Ray Main/Mainstream; 23 Octopus Publishing Group/Marianne Majerus; 24–25 Deidi Von Schaewen; 25r Red Cover/Graham Atkins-Hughes; 27, 28 Ray Main/Mainstream; 29 Andreas von Einsiedel; 30 Camera Press; 31 Red Cover/Graham Atkins–Hughes; 32 International Interiors/Paul Ryan/architects: Stamberg & Aferiat; 33 Red Cover/Verity Welstead; 34 Taverne Agency/Alexander van Berge; 35a International Interiors/Paul Ryan; 35b Agence Top/Pascal Hinous; 36 Verne/Houses & Interiors; 37 International Interiors/Paul Ryan; 38 Elle Decoration/Mark Williams; 39r Kettle's Yard, University of Cambridge; 41 Narratives/Jan Baldwin; 42 Verne/Houses & Interiors; 43 Narratives/Jan Baldwin; 44 Arcaid/Alan Weintraub; 45a Ray Main/Mainstream; 45b Abode; 46 Camera Press; 47 Octopus Publishing Group/Simon Upton; 48, 49 Deidi Von Schaewen; 50 World of Interiors/James Merrell; 51 Verne/Houses & Interiors; 52 Kettles Yard, University of Cambridge; 53a & b Andreas Von Einsiedel; 54 Camera Press; 55 Franca Speranza/Verne; 56 International Interiors/Paul Ryan; 57 Deidi Von Schaewen; 58–59 Narratives/Jan Baldwin; 59r International Interiors/Paul Ryan; 61 Abode; 63 Red Cover/Ken Hayden; 64 Interior Archive/Fritz von der Schulenburg; 65 Arcaid/Alberto Piovano; 66 Interior Archive/Fritz von der Schulenburg/antique dealer: Axel Vervoordt; 67a Kettles Yard, University of Cambridge; 67b International Interiors/Paul Ryan/designer: Kriistina Ratia; 68 Kunstkammer Georg Laue, Munich; 69, 70 Ray Main/Mainstream/designer: Ian Manking; 71 International Interiors/Paul Ryan; 72 Interior Archive/Fritz von der Schulenburg; 73 Interior Archive/Tim Beddow; 74 Deidi Von Schaewen; 75 Ray Main/Mainstream/designer: L Llewelyn-Bowen; 76 Interior Archive/Fritz von der Schulenberg; 77 International Interiors/Paul Ryan; 78–79 Deidi Von Schaewen; 79r Elle Decoration; 81 Ray Main/Mainstream; 82, 83 Deidi Von Schaewen; 84l Camera Press/designer: Max Jourdan; 84r View/Alan Crow/architects: 51% Studios; 85 Red Cover/Mark York; 86 Narratives/Peter Dixon; 87a Andreas von Einsiedel/Sue Timney Fowler; 87b Narratives/Jan Baldwin; 88 Interior Archive/Andrew Wood/stylist: Polly Dickens; 89l Deidi Von Schaewen; 89r Verne/P Vonck; 90 Taverne Agency; 91 International Interiors/Paul Ryan/designer: Ivan Chermayeff; 92–3 Interior Archive/Henry Wilson/designer: Oxley; 93r Arcaid/Trevor Main/Belle/architects: Daryl Jackson; 95 Ray Main/Mainstream; 96 View/Philip Bier/architect: Fiona Ashford; 97 Ray Main/Mainstream/light designer: Bruce Munro, 98 Ray Main/Mainstream; 99 Arcaid/Richard Bryant/architects: Tsao & McKown; 100 Red Cover/Huntley Hedworth; 101a Narratives/Jan Baldwin; 101b Interior Archive/Andrew Wood; 102 View/Dennis Gilbert/architects: Chance De Silva; 103 Arcaid/Trevor Main/Belle/architects: Daryl Jackson; 104 Sebastian Hedgecoe; 105, 106 View/Dennis Gilbert; 107 Deidi Von Schaewen; 108–9 View/Dennis Gilbert/architects: Chance de Silva; 109br Camera Press; 111 Deidi Von Schaewen; 112 The Energy Bank; 113 Interior Archive/Ed Reeve/architects: Adjaye and Russell; 114 Artur/designer: Boris Sipek; 115 Ray Main/Mainstream; 116 Verne; 117a International Interiors/Paul Ryan/designer: Kevin Gray; 117b Agence Top/Roland Beaufre; 118 Interior Archive/Edina van der Wyck; 119 International Interiors/Paul Ryan/designer: Marjolyn Wittich; 120al Elle Decoration/Mark Williams; 120ar Ray Main/Mainstream; 120bl Narratives/Jan Baldwin; 120 br Interior Archive/Henry Wilson; 121r Ray Main/Mainstream; 121a Deidi Von Schaewen; 121bl View/Dennis Gilbert; 132, 135 Narratives/Jan Baldwin.

DATE DUE

MAR 26, 2003		
MAR 28 2003	SEP 18 2003	
	OCT 28 2003	
APR 14 2003	NOV 05 2003	
	NOV 24 2003	
MAY 12 2003		
JUN 11 2003	DEC 22 2003	
	JAN 26 2004	
JUN 26 2003		
JUL 23 2003	MAY 04 2004	
	SEP 07 2004	
AUG 04 2003	SEP 28 2004	
AUG 25 2003		
SEP 02 2003		
GAYLORD		PRINTED IN U.S.A.